The Girl at the Orga Privat

German Studies in Australia and Aotearoa New Zealand

Edited by Professor Tim Mehigan FAHA, University of Queensland

Vol. 23

PETER LANG
Oxford - Berlin - Bruxelles - Chennai - Lausanne - New York

The Girl at the Orga Privat

A Short Novel from Berlin

Translation and Introduction by
Geoff Wilkes

PETER LANG
Oxford - Berlin - Bruxelles - Chennai - Lausanne - New York

Bibliographic information published by the Deutsche Nationalbibliothek.
The German National Library lists this publication in the German National Bibliography; detailed bibliographic data is available on the Internet at http://dnb.d-nb.de.

A catalogue record for this book is available from the British Library.

Library of Congress Cataloging-in-Publication Data

Names: Braune, Rudolf, author. | Wilkes, Geoff (Lecturer in German), translator, editor.
Title: The girl at the Orga Privat : a short novel from Berlin / [Rudolf Braune] ; [edited and translated by] Geoff Wilkes.
Other titles: Mädchen an der Orga Privat. English
Description: Oxford ; New York : Peter Lang, 2024. | Series: German studies in Australia and Aotearoa New Zealand, 0171-6867 ; volume no. 23 | Includes bibliographical references and index.
Identifiers: LCCN 2024031373 (print) | LCCN 2024031374 (ebook) | ISBN 9781803745329 (paperback) | ISBN 9781803745336 (ebook) | ISBN 9781803745343 (epub)
Subjects: LCGFT: Social problem fiction. | Novels.
Classification: LCC PT2603.R384 M313 2024 (print) | LCC PT2603.R384 (ebook) | DDC 833/.912—dc23/eng/20240719
LC record available at https://lccn.loc.gov/2024031373
LC ebook record available at https://lccn.loc.gov/2024031374

First English translation of Rudolf Braune's *Das Mädchen an der Orga Privat* (Frankfurt am Main: Societäts-Verlag, 1930).

Cover image: 'Woman at Typewriter with Notepad.' Photo by Willem van de Poll, 1931. Held by Dutch National Archives. In the public domain, sourced from Wikipedia Commons.
Cover design by Peter Lang Group AG

ISSN 0171-6867
ISBN 978-1-80374-532-9 (print)
ISBN 978-1-80374-533-6 (ePDF)
ISBN 978-1-80374-534-3 (ePub)
DOI 10.3726/b21958

Published by Peter Lang Ltd, Oxford, United Kingdom
info@peterlang.com – www.peterlang.com

This publication has been peer reviewed.

Contents

Introduction

The Girl at the What?

I should begin by explaining that Orga Privat was a brand of typewriter which was manufactured (originally by Bing Co. in Nuremberg) between 1923 and 1950. Although I remember seeing one among the equipment of a provincial archive in Mecklenburg in about 1990, I presume that by now the Orga Privat survives only in museums.[1] A twenty-first-century successor to Bing Co., BING Power Systems LLC, makes components for motor vehicles.

Rudolf Braune's *The Girl at the Orga Privat* (*Das Mädchen an der Orga Privat*, 1930), was probably the first novel in German to include a brand-name product in the title. The only other such novel of which I am aware is Walter Kempowski's *Tadellöser & Wolff* (1971), which alludes to the Loeser & Wolff tobacco company; Florian Illies's best-selling *Generation Golf* (2000), which refers to the Volkswagen Golf, is a memoir rather than a novel.

Rudolf Braune

Born in Dresden on 16 February 1907, Braune was a young revolutionary in a hurry. After leaving school to begin an apprenticeship in the book trade, in 1923 he joined a theatrical troupe called 'The Proletarian

1 An Orga Privat is one of the exhibits at the 'Museum Factory' in the provincial German town of Pritzwalk, approximately eighty miles northwest of Berlin. See <https://nat.museum-digital.de/object/200589?navlang=de>, accessed 9 May 2024.

Audience', which chose Ernst Toller's *Transfiguration* (1919) for its debut performance and concluded that performance with the actors urging the theatregoers to join them in singing 'The Internationale'. In 1925 Braune cofounded a magazine for young people called *MOB*, claiming in the introduction to the first issue that the editors were opposed to 'the fat bourgeois' and that they counted Lenin, Georg Büchner, Paul Klee, Otto Dix and Charlie Chaplin among their idols. The magazine published articles with titles such as 'Christ on the Cross Is a Petit-Bourgeois Concept' and 'Notes of a Factory Worker' as well as a translation of a letter from Lenin to Maxim Gorky. *MOB* was suppressed after five issues, following intervention by the police, and by the authorities in the schools at which the magazine was partly aimed.

Braune visited the Soviet Union in mid-1925 and moved from Dresden to Düsseldorf about a year later. There he became a member of the Communist Party of Germany and began working for a Party newspaper called *Freedom*. He had a particular interest in the cinema, producing more than two hundred film reviews for *Freedom* over about three years, but he also wrote fiction, publishing his first novel as a serial in *Freedom* in June and July 1928. This was *The Battle on the Kille*, the 'Kille' being a stretch of high ground between Essen and Hagen. *The Girl at the Orga Privat* was the first novel by Braune to appear in book form. He did not live to see the publication of his next novel, *Young People in the City*, at the end of 1932, as he had drowned while swimming in the Rhine near Düsseldorf on 12 June that year. He was twenty-five years old.

Braune's premature death, and the fact that his communist beliefs led the Nazis to suppress his works, at least partly explain the lack of personal and literary documents providing information about his life and his career as an author. For example, very few letters written by or to Braune are known to be extant, and no drafts, manuscripts, proofs or other versions of his journalistic or literary publications appear to have survived. Between 1949 and 1990, the memory of Braune's works was kept alive largely in the German Democratic Republic, with reissues of his three novels, radio and television versions of *The Girl at the Orga Privat*, and television and film versions of *Young People in the City*. However, *The Girl at the Orga Privat* has been reissued three times in the twenty-first century, most recently by the Jaron Press in Berlin in 2022.

The secondary literature about the novel is rather limited. The scholarly reception of Braune's work began in the German Democratic Republic, but mostly offered formulaic assessments along the lines of Friedrich Albrecht's characterization of Braune in 1975 as one of 'those young authors of bourgeois origin who, during the Weimar period, formed the new generation of the proletarian-revolutionary literary movement'.[2] As far as I am aware, the first substantial scholarly interpretations of *The Girl at the Orga Privat* to appear outside the GDR were those by Christa Jordan and Renny Harrigan in 1988;[3] these remain the most detailed and useful commentaries on the novel, and I will refer to them in my own analysis below. The only book about Braune, published by Martin Hollender in 2004,[4] is very informative about the author's life and bibliography, but does not discuss his fiction in any depth.

2 Friedrich Albrecht, *Deutsche Schriftsteller in der Entscheidung: Wege zur Arbeiterklasse 1918–1933* (Berlin and Weimar: Aufbau, 1975), 333. The translation here, and all other translations from the German in this Introduction, are my own.

3 See Christa Jordan, *Zwischen Zerstreuung und Berauschung. Die Angestellten in der Erzählprosa am Ende der Weimarer Republik* (Frankfurt am Main: Peter Lang, 1988), 219–40 & 366–9; and Renny Harrigan, 'Novellistic Representation of *die Berufstätige* during the Weimar Republic', *Women in German Yearbook* 4 (1988), 97–124. Some other scholars have discussed the *Girl at the Orga Privat* in passing, for example Vibeke Rützou Petersen, *Women and Modernity in Weimar Germany: Reality and Its Representation in Popular Fiction* (New York: Berghahn, 2001), 15, 33, 47–8, 79 & 152.

4 Martin Hollender, *'eine gefährliche Unruhe im Blut ...' Rudolf Braune: Schriftsteller und Journalist* (Düsseldorf: Grupello, 2004). This is the source for my account of Braune's life above. Hollender has also edited a selection of Braune's shorter texts: *Rudolf Braune Lesebuch* (Düsseldorf: Edition Virgines, 2015).

The Girl at the Orga Privat

The novel's main character is the eighteen-year-old Erna Halbe, who leaves her provincial hometown to take a job as stenotypist with 'Iron Processing Co.' in Berlin. Her colleagues dub her 'The Girl at the Orga Privat' when she is given an inferior old typewriter of that brand to work on while better and newer Remingtons are being repaired. *The Girl at the Orga Privat* is therefore one of several novels published during the last years of the Weimar Republic dealing partly or wholly with women who worked in offices and shops. These novels included Vicki Baum's *Grand Hotel* (1929), Irmgard Keun's *Gilgi, One of Us* (1931) and Gabriele Tergit's *Käsebier Takes Berlin* (1931). As the female characters were usually quite young, the novels often had the word 'Girl' in the title, for example Josefine Lederer's *The Girl George* (1928), Keun's *The Artificial Silk Girl* (1932) and Christa Anita Brück's *A Girl With Power of Attorney* (1932). Women white-collar workers were also staple characters in late Weimar films, such as *People on Sunday* (1930), *The Private Secretary* (1931) and *Wrong Number, Fräulein* (1932).

These novels and films reflected a number of significant developments in German society after the Great War. Firstly, there was the emergence of the so-called 'New Woman', a term which encompassed not only material circumstances such as women's increased participation in the public sphere (for example in white-collar employment specifically, paid work generally, university education, cultural life and politics), but also attitudinal shifts such as greater tolerance towards sex outside marriage, abortion and lesbianism (although these shifts were not necessarily mirrored in the relevant legislation), as well as more prosaic changes in feminine fashions such as shorter hemlines and shorter hairstyles. Depictions and discussions of New Women in literature and cinema (and elsewhere) often paid particular attention to their sex lives and their clothes. Secondly, the authors' and filmmakers' interest in offices and shops resonated with the intellectual and artistic concept of 'New Objectivity', which was formulated in the early 1920s, and which frequently sought its subject matter in the mundane, famous examples being Egon Erwin Kisch's descriptions of locales including a steelworks, a fishing village and a morgue in the reportages collected in *The Racing Reporter* (1924), and Walther Ruttmann's montage of scenes from streets, workplaces, cafés and so on in the film *Berlin: The Symphony of the Metropolis* (1927). Finally, the Weimar Republic saw the rise of Berlin – which of course had only become the national capital with the unification of Germany in 1871 – demographically, economically and culturally to the status of a European city comparable in significance to Paris and London. Two indications of Berlin's cultural importance, at least, during the Weimar Republic are the facts that most of the novels and films which I mentioned in the previous paragraph are set wholly or partly in that city (and *Gilgi, One of Us* ends with the protagonist boarding a train for the capital), and that all of the five authors mentioned above lived and/or published in Berlin for at least some of the late 1920s and early 1930s.

Although *The Girl at the Orga Privat* is reasonably typical of the late Weimar novels with female white-collar protagonists, it is comparatively unusual in that it was written from a left-wing viewpoint, and also in that it was written by a man. Turning firstly to Braune's political position: he emphasizes Erna's working-class origins from the outset, noting in the second paragraph of the narrative that she 'comes from a poky little industrial town near Korbetha in Central Germany', where '[h]er father works in the mine', and where she was 'the fourth of eleven children'. This pedigree evidently equips Erna to deal with the emergencies and problems of life. When she arrives at Iron Processing Co. on her first morning to the news that one of her colleagues has just fainted, only she has the initiative and the knowledge to tell the others to splash water on the young woman's face and open a window. And after Erna has spent only a few days at her new job, her colleagues have rather implausibly developed the habit of asking her advice on various personal matters, because she 'says things so simply and sensibly, she doesn't make a big fuss, but just listens carefully and then works out something'. Braune also identifies two of the dozen other women in Erna's office as 'from a humble background', and as therefore admirable. The first is the train driver's daughter Elsbeth Siewertz, who 'doesn't put up with anything from [her boss] Lortzing or even [his boss] Siodmak', and who is 'walking straight ahead through her young life and knows exactly what she wants'. The second is Otti Heynicke, who 'was brought up in [the suburb of] Wedding, where the workers live', and is unmoved by her colleagues' pretensions to bourgeois social status.

Having established Erna's working-class credentials, Braune makes her the key figure in a strike at Iron Processing Co. She works out that Trude Leussner (the woman who fainted) is ill because she has made several illegal attempts to abort a pregnancy resulting from an affair with Lortzing, and when Trude is sacked 'for inadequate work' Erna persuades all the other young women in the office to withdraw their labour. They elect an 'action committee' which includes Erna and Elsbeth, and they demand that Trude be reinstated, and that they all be paid at the legal rates.

Given Braune's strong left-wing propensities, readers might expect the strike to be a resounding success, but this is not the case. Although Erna has the working-class smarts which make her 'the soul of the struggle', she commits a tactical error on the second day by leaving the office unoccupied at lunchtime, so that she and her colleagues are locked out, and in danger of being replaced by new hires. That danger is only averted because Trude dies in hospital the same day, which prompts Siodmak to refrain from mass sackings in order to avoid scandal. But the young women return to work, nothing more is heard of their pay claim, and Iron Processing Co. makes no admissions about Trude's pregnancy: Siodmak tells Erna that 'you can rest assured that both Herr Lortzing and I acted perfectly correctly. In every respect'. And Erna herself is fired, albeit with a full month's salary and a good reference, because (as Siodmak says) the firm's 'prestige' in its employees' eyes requires this.

Christa Jordan argues that this rather muted ending reflects 'sociohistorical realities' of the Weimar Republic which make it impossible for the novel to offer 'a credible, optimistic prospect of a socialist or communist future'.[5] While this may be so, I would suggest that Braune is not immediately concerned with such a prospect, but instead characterizes the strike as a first lesson in collective action. The narrative makes a number of comments about how even 'small campaign[s]' such as Erna and her colleagues are waging can 'grow overnight if their leaders are clear and confident', and how '[t]he world's suffering isn't so great when the

5 Jordan, *Zwischen Zerstreuung und Berauschung*, 223–4.

working people help each other, when comradeship and resistance grow within their ranks'. The strike is described repeatedly in terms of 'fighting' and 'the battle' (which I have translated from 'kämpfen' and 'Kampf' in the original German text). And when Erna leaves Iron Processing Co. at the end of the novel, Braune asserts rather vaingloriously that her former colleagues will remember her 'with secret pride and undisguised love. [...] New girls will come into the office, and they'll all be told little stories about Erna Halbe, little things she said, she'll continue to live among them. [...] What she did won't be forgotten, it will grow and grow.'

In presenting the strike as he does, Braune takes up a position in the sociopolitical debates of the Weimar Republic which was perhaps most famously articulated by Siegfried Kracauer. This was that various processes of rationalization in the workplace had reduced white-collar employees to much the same economic status as blue-collar workers, so that the former had become heavily invested psychologically in largely meaningless markers of their middle-class social status. In *Die Angestellten* (*The Salaried Masses*, 1930), Kracauer argues that 'at the present time, large sectors of the population actually take such circumstances as that their salary is paid monthly [rather than weekly], that supposedly they work with their heads [rather than with their hands], and some other similarly inconsequential factors, as proof of their bourgeois existence, although it is no longer bourgeois at all'.[6]

In this context, the story of how the miner's-daughter-turned-stenotypist Erna persuades her more genteel colleagues to strike for Trude's reinstatement and better pay functions not only as a lesson about collective action, but also as a lesson about the necessity of white-collar workers recognizing their gentility as a barrier to collective action. That barrier is indicated, for example, by the way Erna's coworker Lieselotte Kries demurs at the strike as 'practically Bolshevism', and 'the kind of thing the Communists and people like that do'. And the deficiencies of the petit-bourgeois mentality are made more than clear when Erna discusses the chances of industrial action at her office with Fritz Drehkopf, a mechanic she takes up with soon after her arrival in Berlin. Fritz declares that: 'Most office workers are

6 Siegfried Kracauer, *Die Angestellten: Aus dem neuesten Deutschland*, rev. edn (1930; repr., Frankfurt am Main: Suhrkamp, 1971), 81.

shit,[7] but there's always a first time.' Later in this discussion, Fritz complains that Erna's colleagues lack 'class consciousness', and she agrees.[8]

Braune emphasizes that the young women's misguided ideas are influenced by their enthusiastic participation in the consumer culture of the Weimar Republic. On Erna's first morning at Iron Processing Co., a colleague relieves the monotony of typing for everybody by whistling popular songs (she begins with the suggestively titled 'What Are You Doing With Your Knee, Hans Dear?' – in which a young woman complains about one Hans's inept dancing). This performance is followed by a general conversation 'about men and about dancing, [...] about cinemas and about clothes', and later when Erna and some of her coworkers eat lunch at a cheap refectory, the female guests there talk of '[n]ew movies and the price of clothes'. Erna has already demonstrated her own interest in films by attending a screening of Norma Talmadge's *Kiki* the previous evening. And although a colleague mocks Erna's out-of-season blouse when she returns to the office after lunch, she impresses everybody the next morning by appearing in a 'stylish dress and [...] wonderful hat', which she fashioned overnight from her Sunday best and an outmoded soft bonnet that she had only put in her travelling suitcase to separate layers of clothes.

Braune treats the poor-girl-makes-good plot of *Kiki* (in which a Parisian newspaper seller marries an affluent theatre owner) rather ironically: 'She's a real working-class girl, who has to make her own way and carves out a place for herself. [...] Kiki as a variety girl and Kiki as a lady. Isn't life wonderful in this cinema? You get to see everything, life out there in the world, life here in the city. Kiki meets a really classy guy, and good luck to her.' The narrative also deals dismissively with the other young women's delight in Erna's revamped dress and hat, seeing it as evidence of their superficial thinking. They 'change their opinion of this unprepossessing little girl from the provinces quickly and completely, although they don't think much about their change of attitude. What registers with them is that

7 'Die Angestellten sind ja im allgemeinen jämmerliche Scheißkerle', in the original German.

8 Jordan also notes the novel's emphasis on the discontinuity between the white-collar workers' 'proletarian status' and their 'false [...] petit-bourgeois consciousness' (*Zwischen Zerstreuung und Berauschung*, 230).

something new has happened. They look with their eyes and listen with their ears and smell with their noses, anything beyond that is somebody else's problem.' In other words, Braune suggests that the consumer culture of popular songs and films and clothes is designed to discourage the young office workers from pondering their precarious economic situation by, for example, offering them fantasies of poor women who marry rich men, or producing constantly changing fashions which position clothes as markers of social status. This idea too was articulated by Kracauer, who characterizes the Weimar Republic's mass culture as one of 'distraction' ('Zerstreuung'). Kracauer was particularly interested in the cinema, which he describes as 'justifying the existing order' by dulling the audience's mind with 'the glittering simulacrum of the supposed heights of society'.[9]

It is also worth noting the women's sexual relationships, which are so numerous that I have space to mention and comment only on some of them. Trude of course has the affair with Lortzing (who is married) which leads to the strike. Lieselotte (who is married) also has an affair with Lortzing as well as with Wolf, the brother of her colleague Erika Tümmler. Erika has an affair not with Lortzing, but with the other boss, Siodmak (who is married). The seventeen-year-old Grete Theier has an affair with a bank clerk called Einsiedel, who is 'a little over forty'. Erna sleeps with Fritz the fourth time she sees him, which is only the second time she speaks with him. And Otti has a relationship with an unnamed truck driver and shows her pride in her working-class origins by letting him pick her up from the office in his truck, onto which she 'swings herself up quickly and elegantly'.

The most significant relationships are those with the older and more affluent men (such as Lortzing, Siodmak and Einsiedel), from which the young women derive significant material benefits. And the women discuss these affairs mainly in materialistic terms. Sometimes the benefits are quite substantial, for example when Grete confides to Erna that she hopes Einsiedel (who has already bought her 'a big fur coat') will 'pay for her to have her own apartment'. Sometimes the relationships serve to supplement the young women's mostly meagre salaries, as when Erna expresses disapproval of Erika's affair with Siodmak, and her colleague Lotte Weissbach

9 Kracauer, *Die Angestellten*, 99.

says: 'Erna, dear, you're a nice girl, but please just think sometime about how you're going to live in Berlin on your hundred and twenty marks, or whatever they're paying you.' And in one scene the narrative treats relationships as a matter of bare survival, though not relationships with better-paid men, specifically. When an unnamed guest at the refectory starts crying because she is about to lose her job, another young woman asks whether she has a boyfriend; a male guest objects to this and a third woman says: 'I'd look for a boyfriend, sooner than starving to death.'

Erna does not seek any financial gain from her relationship with the mechanic Fritz. And as her attitude to Erika and Siodmak suggests, she is inclined to criticize her colleagues' affairs. During the discussion at the refectory, she recalls the stricter morality of her working-class upbringing: 'Back home, things sometimes turned bad between boys and girls, but if a girl was expecting a baby then there had to be a marriage, otherwise the boy would have had something to deal with.' But after Erna realizes that Trude is pregnant and looking for an abortion, she becomes more sympathetic. When a doctor she consults deprecates Trude's thoughtlessness, Erika defends her: 'A twenty-year-old girl [...] who sees nice things all around her, and whose girlfriends are having a good time and who can't get married in the foreseeable future, is she supposed to just sit around and wait, with her hundred and thirty marks?' Erna's final viewpoint thus reinforces Braune's ideas about the white-collar mentality. The young women's affairs are largely a way of affirming their bourgeois status in a society which gives them little economic security. And, recalling Kracauer's analysis of consumer culture, the 'big fur coat[s]' and other 'nice things' which the more affluent men provide offer 'the glittering simulacrum of the supposed heights of society'.

I noted above that *The Girl at the Orga Privat* is comparatively unusual among the novels of its time and with its subject matter in having been written by a man. This may explain the fact that, although its analysis of female office workers is fairly subtle in sociopolitical terms, its representation of women is often insensitive, sexualized and paternalistic. Braune's lack of sensitivity is most obvious in the development of Trude's story. For most of the novel, she is a sympathetic figure whose pregnancy and death show the harsh medical and social realities which sometimes underlie the fleeting psychological and material consolations of an affair with the boss.

But after Trude's death these realities fade from view. When Siodmak assures Erna quite falsely that he and Lortzing always acted with complete propriety towards Trude, she looks out the window without challenging him, or even answering him. And when Erna tells the others that she is leaving and they are going back to work, she does not mention Trude, and neither do they. But Erna realizes that the threat of scandal after Trude's death is what prompted Siodmak to sack only her and not the others, and she remarks to Erika privately and bloodlessly: 'Trude's death probably saved us.' In other words, the story which at the beginning was an egregious case of what we would now call workplace sexual harassment is reduced at the end to a plot device.

Braune's sexualization of the young women is particularly – and perhaps surprisingly – apparent in his descriptions of Erna. On her second morning in Berlin, Erna inspects her naked body in the mirror of her rented room, with the narrative noting among other things how '[h]er cute little breasts stand out cheekily from her body, pushing upwards slightly'. Later, Erna is examined under the male gaze of Fritz, who approves of her 'wonderful body, [...] strong, well-formed and a little bit plump, just the way he likes it'. There is also a voyeuristic element in the scene where Erna and Erika, who are alone in the office late on the first day of the strike, embrace: 'Erna lifts her right hand from Erika's shoulder, gently strokes her friend's face, her hair, tousles it tenderly, runs her fingers through it and draws Erika's head towards her, close, very close. Erika [...] lifts the little girl's face close to hers and gives her a rough, strong kiss.' And Braune's characterizations of the supposedly more attractive women can become ridiculous, as with Erika: 'The slightly slanted eyes are shimmering a light green, transparent, clear, there's something enticing about them. Young men have looked into these eyes and then cried because they couldn't get what they wanted from this girl. They wrote stupid letters and did stupid things and were never able to forget Erika.' Even the comparatively unimportant Hilde, a guest at the refectory, is a 'beautiful girl' whose 'clearly defined mouth curves forward, [with] long lashes cover[ing] her lovely eyes,' at whom Erna looks 'in quiet admiration'.

The narrative's paternalism is evident in the repeated descriptions of Erna as 'a little girl' or 'the little one' or 'the little typist'.[10] These descriptions begin in the first paragraph and are extended to seven of Erna's twelve colleagues. Fritz is equally patronizing, for example, when he and Erna are discussing the possibility of a strike at Iron Processing Co., and he says: 'If something new happens, you've got to tell me about it at once. Then I'll tell you what you've got to do.' Moreover, Erna complies. After the women withdraw their labour, she tells Erika that she will be 'meeting Fritz' to seek his advice. And although Fritz is arrested for creating a disturbance at his workplace before Erna can do this, she still takes him as her guide, arguing fiercely against some of her colleagues who want to stop the strike partly because she is embarrassed to think 'what [...] Fritz Drehkopf [would] say if he heard how shamefully the struggle had ended'.[11]

Having noted at the outset that the company that manufactured the Orga Privat in the 1920s has a successor which makes automobile components today, I would conclude by suggesting that Braune's novel also has both a historical and a contemporary significance. On one hand, *The Girl at the Orga Privat* is a novel of its time and place: the last years of Weimar Germany. Erna works on what we now call a 'manual' typewriter, goes to what we now term a 'silent' film, and moves around a rapidly expanding Berlin in which the suburb of Wilmersdorf (about five miles from the city centre) still has 'uncultivated building land'. Erna's and her colleagues' jobs, their relationships with men and their interest in consumer culture are typical of the so-called New Woman who was a staple figure in the media of the Weimar Republic. And the novel's analysis of the female white-collar workers' socioeconomic position and class consciousness clearly reflects ideas which were current in the Communist Party of Germany and elsewhere, although those ideas were not represented very strongly in literary fiction. On the other hand, much in what Braune describes, and in the way

10 The key word in the German text is of course 'klein' or the associated adjectival noun.

11 Both Renny Harrigan and Christa Jordan refer briefly to aspects of Braune's sexism – such as his 'objectification of female sexuality' through Fritz in particular (Harrigan, 'Novellistic Representation', 103), and his 'condescending masculine tone' more generally (Jordan, *Zwischen Zerstreuung und Berauschung*, 238) – but they do not discuss the issue in depth.

he describes it, will be recognizable to twenty-first-century readers familiar with precarious employment, with spurious markers of bourgeois status (such as the vaguely entrepreneurial title of 'independent contractor' which is bestowed on low-paid workers in the 'gig economy'), and with politically tendentious mass culture. In particular, Trude's ill-fated affair with Lortzing and Braune's pronounced and unconscious sexism have obvious parallels in the contemporary era of contentious abortion laws and of '#MeToo'.

Translator's Note

This is the first translation of *Das Mädchen an der Orga Privat* into English, and only the third into any language, following Serbo-Croatian and Hungarian translations published in 1931 and 2021, respectively. I did not encounter any very difficult linguistic issues in Braune's text. Cultural references such as those to the film *Kiki* and the song 'What Are You Doing With Your Knee, Hans Dear?' were authentic, and presented no particular translation problems. The only changes I made were to add unobtrusive glosses where I thought that something familiar to the novel's original readers might need clarification for later readers. For example, a sentence early in the German text has Erna walking past, simply, 'Wertheim und Tietz'; I translated this as 'the Wertheim and Tietz department stores'.

Copies of the first edition of *The Girl at the Orga Privat* seem to be unobtainable on the antiquarian book market and are held by only a handful of libraries worldwide, none of which were readily accessible to me. My source text for this translation was therefore a scanned copy of the first edition which is available on the website of the University of Cologne.[1] That edition presents one continuous text, with nothing whatsoever – no chapter headings, blank lines, asterisks etc. – to indicate individual chapters or sections of any kind. Therefore my translation is also a continuous text.

1 I am grateful to Dr Christian Romuss for locating that copy <https://uni-koeln.de/phil-fak/deutsch/aleki/schatzbehalter/inhalt/B/braune_maedchen_orga.pdf>, and for his research and editorial assistance with various aspects of my translation.

The Girl at the Orga Privat

A Short Novel from Berlin

BY RUDOLF BRAUNE

One morning in the spring of 1928, a young girl arrives on the Leipzig train at Anhalt Station in Berlin. Nobody is waiting for her. Nobody pays any attention to her in the confusion of this workaday Berlin morning, beneath the smoke of a damp, miserable sky. She's carrying a suitcase which seems to be very heavy, because every now and then she switches it to her other hand. The girl walks slowly with short, swinging strides, looking with tired, grumpy eyes at the businesslike scurrying of the railway officials, shop assistants, newspaper sellers, workers and travellers. Just as she's leaving the sooty station building, the rainclouds part and the puddles on the asphalt light up. A dull gleam slides across the grey façades of the buildings, jumps over the signs with the businesses' names, past bay windows and faux balconies, and springs across the street to this little girl, who'll stand for some minutes at the exit from Anhalt Station before she disappears into the confusion of the city. Her suitcase is on the ground beside her, her large hands are in the pockets of her coat, which is speckled with brown. Erna Halbe is seeing Berlin for the first time.

She comes from a poky little industrial town near Korbetha in Central Germany. Her father works in the mine, and she – the fourth of eleven children – learned typing and stenography, and worked in a lawyer's office for four years. She couldn't take the cramped conditions, the endless bickering and commotion in her parents' home anymore. A few days ago, after lots of unsuccessful efforts and applications, she got a letter of acceptance from Berlin at last. A hundred and thirty marks gross per month, the firm wrote, starting on Wednesday morning at nine o'clock.

It was her first long journey.

First I've got to find myself a room, she decides. She goes back into the station and deposits her suitcase in the luggage office.

She travelled all night, half-asleep the whole time, in a smoky compartment. On the cold, deserted platform at Bitterfeld Station she ate a hot sausage, that was her only sustenance on the journey, now her stomach is rumbling.

Nothing about her shows that she's never been in this city before. She walks slowly through the bustling streets over to Potsdam Square, quite curious, looking at everything carefully, but not gaping at all. The girl's inadequate spring coat makes her look even more nondescript than she is to begin with. Her thin legs stick out oddly below the coat, revealing a slightly knock-kneed tendency. Erna is aware of this, but it doesn't bother her particularly. Her life is just beginning, and lots of things are going to change. She takes a good look at her reflection in the window of a big delicatessen. Well really, what kind of face is that? More or less everything about it is messed up. Her nose is too big, her red hair is too lifeless, her mouth is too full. A kind of seam runs along her chin, a scar from a brawl with some boys years ago. She can't even find anything good about her high, broad forehead, the nice long curve, the bumps projecting over the eyes. She doesn't think any of that is particularly worth mentioning, the most she does is to note the soft veil of freckles which runs across her forehead, ending with a few big, light-coloured spots on her nose. She pulls a face at her reflection; while she's not vain, she does still feel a certain admiration for special and valuable things, and she has clear, simple ideas about what's beautiful and what's ugly.

At that moment, Erna senses that somebody is looking at her. She's rarely wrong about that, and she's startled, because she's just pulled such a horrible face. She wants to walk on quickly, but she still can't stop herself turning her head to the side for an instant. And in fact, three paces away from the window, a young worker in a blue overall jacket is standing with his hands in his pockets and winking at her as he laughs. She walks on quickly. Well, at least he didn't say anything to her, because she wants nothing to do with these street pick-ups. She knows how easily a girl who works for her living can slip up, she's careful, she'll marry a good man someday, they'll have children and they'll have to work, she's looking for a minimum of happiness. She doesn't let her feelings run away with her, because she knows about life already, the darkest side of life.

Erna walks down Leipzig Street, past the Wertheim and Tietz department stores, across the Spittel Market, over to Alexander Square. Without asking, without any local knowledge, she makes her way to the eastern part of the city without major mistakes or detours. Her hunger returns, and she sits down at a little pub in Landsberg Street. Delivery vehicles are driving past outside, heavy trucks, a cheerful car painted in the bright colours of Shell Oil. Lots of workers, women doing their midday shopping, children going home from school, a newspaper seller calling out the headlines. The sun is drying out the wet pavement. Erna buys a buttered roll, pays ten pfennigs, and goes on. She walks along a railway embankment, the trains are heading for Silesia Station, she can hear factory sirens, it seems to be lunchtime already, her legs are hurting. She's tired. She only pays attention to the little signs hanging in the windows of lots of buildings:

FURNISHED ROOM

TO LET

She's never had furnished lodgings before. She's assuming twenty-five marks per month, that's how much she can afford. She'll be spending all her salary, because of course they won't pay her the whole hundred and thirty marks, unemployment insurance and health insurance will be deducted. She's got to eat, she's got to buy clothes and shoes, and those aren't the only pressing expenses she has.

She really likes the look of the corner building in Rüdersdorf Street. The sign says 'Third Floor', which has an endless row of windows that all look the same, with nothing to break the monotony. But they catch the sun! Inside, on the ground floor, the children are rampaging about. A woman shouts something down to them over the banister. Erna climbs each flight of stairs slowly and deliberately, raising her head from time to time to listen, or to take a look at the next floor. She feels like she's going to the dentist. There are six families living up on the third floor. Which one will have the room to rent? Unsure, she reads the names on the doors. A woman with her sleeves rolled up comes down from the fourth floor.

'That'll be the Zimmermanns.'

The woman from the fourth floor stays there, curious.

Erna rings the bell. A fat, slatternly woman opens up. There's smoke coming from the kitchen, and lots of clothes hanging in the entryway, those are the first things you see. There's a smell of burnt food.

'This way, Fräulein.'

The door bangs shut. Erna has to walk through a dark hallway, a door creaks open to a gloomy little room.

'Got nice furniture, ain't it? Always quiet here. None of my lodgers has ever complained, the last one lived here for two years, was a classy gentleman, he's left town now to work in construction. Next door, that Frau Kuhlmann, she lets rooms too, well, I'm telling you it's filthy like you wouldn't believe. And she wants forty marks for it! Mine only costs thirty-eight. What with the high prices these days, you got to save everywhere you can. We never had to do it before. But as a widow …'

The old woman talks and talks, sighing whenever she draws breath. She has a whiny, unpleasant voice. Her swollen, red hands are resting on her protuberant stomach.

'I'll call again.'

Erna's stuttering, her face has turned red, and she runs quickly down the stairs.

Behind her, the door shuts with a particularly loud bang.

Oh God! Erna thinks. There was barely room to turn around in that hole, and you couldn't see any of the side which catches the sun. Thirty-eight marks? I've got to find something, I've got to find a room, of course I won't lose heart, it's no big deal, it's better to look for a little longer and find something suitable …

And she's quite right.

She goes into lots of buildings which have the little signs hanging in the windows, she climbs up lots of stairs, and down again, she looks at little attic rooms, dusty parlours, furniture from granddad's day, half-dark chambers. Feeble rays of light push through shutters, illuminating countless swirling dust particles. Cheap china ornaments are arranged picturesquely on little shelves and sills. Prints showing curious events, pictures of bright angels, samplers with moral precepts, group photographs, and again and again the 'Storm-Tossed Ship on the High Seas' hang on the walls. She sees some nicer rooms too, but the prices are unexpectedly high everywhere. Most of the landladies tell long stories about why they have to give up their rooms to strangers, they never had to do it before, but the way things are these days … And their sharp eyes look closely at the little girl standing with her long arms hanging down, looking out of place and a bit anxious in these apartments. They're calculating, sizing Erna up.

As Erna moves further into the proletarian district, the look of the streets changes significantly. The pavement becomes uneven and dotted with puddles, the entrances to the buildings are dark and stuffy. Streets run into other streets, there's no end to them, she becomes disoriented and just follows her nose.

Is this why I came here? she wonders. Notices outlining the 'House Rules' hang in every entry. They didn't have those in the little town she comes from. There are scraps of rubbish lying about, and big cracks in the stairwell windows, parts of the decorative coloured panes have been knocked out and replaced with ordinary window glass. Erna sees all of these things only in passing, she's not very strongly aware of them, but it makes her tired and sad. Once, yesterday, the day before and longer ago, everything was going to be different – Berlin! Berlin! – and that hurts. She pulls her face together, making it smaller, more determined. She won't let them knock her down. And she keeps on looking.

So that's the apartment on the fourth floor. 'Neumann' is the name on the door, no, not on the door, the name has been painted onto the yellow letterbox with ink, or India ink. You can only read it if you stand very close to the door and spell it out. And when Erna knocks, you can only see the outline of the woman who opens the door, too, because she's standing in the dark. Her voice is very young and hesitant.

'Yes, come in, come in … I haven't tidied up at all yet … This is the kitchen, and the next room is the bedroom.'

'And the furnished one?'

'No, I don't have a furnished room to let, that's a mistake. You'll have to live in our bedroom. It's not just a place to sleep, no, you'll be nice and comfortable with us, we're doing this for the first time, because my husband is unemployed, you see.'

The young woman looks at Erna pleadingly, big blue eyes fill out her narrow face, beautiful, soft eyes. The room is warm and bright with afternoon light. The cupboard and the table are tidy, the oven is gleaming, a variety of clean pots are lined up in a neat row. You notice the difference between the bright, inviting, clean kitchen and the dark, dirty stairwell immediately. Two children are crawling around on the floor, an infant is asleep in the woman's arms.

'They're twins.'

A man comes out of the bedroom, dressed only in a shirt and trousers, with wood shavings in his hair, and dirty hands.

'The young lady has come about our bedroom.' The woman looks up anxiously at her husband, he is much taller and looks at them bleakly. He hasn't even said 'Good afternoon.'

'Do you only have two rooms?' Erna asks.

The man swings around, Erna is frightened by the rage in his face.

'Nah', the man says, 'we got a nice villa with a dog kennel and a garden for the children, and we don't need no lodgers! Don't need 'em at all!'

Erna looks at the man with shocked eyes as he disappears back into the bedroom. The woman is crying. The children are playing under the table. Bright clouds are drifting past outside. Erna has a bad taste in her mouth, the kitchen is cold, the apartment is sad, life in Berlin is bitter.

'He's had it, his nerves are gone. Unemployed for ten months and no prospects and no hope. What are we going to do?'

The woman is still young, somewhere between twenty and thirty. She has a beautiful, gentle face, which she's covering with one hand as she cries.

What business does Erna Halbe have here anymore, she's not going to stay, she doesn't want to share somebody else's bedroom, she wants her own furnished room, but some little thing is still keeping her here. She draws up a chair, and Frau Neumann sits down. 'No, it's not for you. I know. My husband wants me to offer it with full board and lodging. Otherwise we won't make any profit. Eighty marks for full board and lodging. That's twenty per week. But how long will it take us to find somebody. And then it probably won't be the right one.' She's not crying anymore, she's taken her hands away from her face. Under her skin you can see little blue veins, they're gathering on her forehead and below her eyes especially. She's not a strong person, and Fate is being damned hard on her. The infant is lying on her chest, it's crying, she unbuttons her blouse and holds the child's big head against her small breast. 'I can stick it out, myself. I can still give the little one milk. He's a boy, you see. But my husband gets so worried. He's a good man, believe me. He's building a rabbit hutch for the landlord at the moment. We're doing it to make the rent!'

'What does your husband do?'

'He makes car bodies. Everybody drives a car, but do you think that means there's work? Can you tell me how that's possible?'

No, Erna can't. But she knows what it's like in the brown-coal mines in Central Germany, she talks about the little town she comes from and about her parents. She asks where Prenzlau Avenue is, where her new firm is supposed to be, she enquires about lots of things in Berlin. Yes, she wants to know everything, but she also wants for Frau Neumann to stop crying, for the woman to forget some things for a while.

'You see, I arrived in Berlin this morning. I thought everything would be much easier. But there are so many people living in the city, and one feels alone and abandoned. Can you understand that? One feels really unhappy and depressed. But I won't let them get me down. The skies will be blue again one day.'

Erna smiles, the infant slurps and suckles, a canary starts whistling loudly. Maybe it's been whistling for a while, but Erna has only just noticed. The husband is working in the next room, hammering and planing …

'Can I come to see you again sometime, Frau Neumann? Maybe on a Sunday afternoon, yes?'

Erna is walking along the street more quickly, the afternoon is short. 'Beauty from Elida.' The girl in the soap advertisement has golden blonde hair, rosy cheeks, shining eyes, sweet breath. That's how you've got to look here, right? You need money for that, you need money for everything. I've got to earn money. Of course, I'll move up soon and earn more, much, much more …

Maybe this isn't the right neighbourhood for her. It's all workers' apartments, she's familiar with those cramped rooms and their scrubbed, cheerless cleanliness, their plain furniture which is still being paid off, and their bare walls. She realizes that nothing decent is likely to be available for under thirty marks. In the end she gets a room at Frau Matschek's on the fourth floor of a big five-story building, but before that she has another strange experience.

Erna turns into Koppen Street, which is right behind Silesia Station, the afternoon is drawing to a close, a dull pink sun is crawling behind a cloud. But maybe it's not a cloud, maybe it's only smoke from the industrial chimneys. Workers are leaving their factories, the streets are full of people, everybody is going home, Erna doesn't have anywhere to live yet. What does that mean: Going home? she wonders. At this time of day Father's coming off shift, and I had to fetch in the coal. So who's fetching in the coal today? Luise or Mother? The planks around the coal heap collapsed again, they'll have to rebuild everything, it's very dirty work.

We didn't have newspaper kiosks at home, no, only in Korbetha, there's one on every corner here, I keep stopping and looking at the photos. Who's that pretty girl? Marion Davies. Oh, right, a girl from Hollywood. I'll go to the movies sometime too. But first I've got to have a room, a room, a room, that'd make quite a nice tune …

She climbs up four flights of stairs, four gloomy floors. The building has a musty smell of children's unwashed clothes and poor food. Always living in a building like this, Erna thinks, no, it makes you miserable, I know what it's like. She wants to turn back, but she goes on nevertheless, tonight she's got to sleep in her own room, peacefully and without any worries.

The name on the door is 'Ziegenbein'. Yes, 'Goat's Leg'.

Erna rings the bell. She rings again. And because nobody opens up, she goes away. She walks down a few steps, then the door up there creaks. She can't see who's standing there, because the building is half-dark, but she can tell by the voice that a young man is talking to her.

'Who do you want to see?'

'Could I speak to Frau Ziegenbein?'

'No, Frau Ziegenbein isn't in.'

Snap. The door's closed.

But it opens again.

'I suppose you've come about the room?'

'Of course.'

'Well, I can show you the room just as well.'

Erna walks up the few steps again, wipes her shoes on the mat and follows the young man into Frau Ziegenbein's apartment, not thinking about anything except how that young man might perhaps be related to Frau Ziegenbein, something which understandably is of interest to Erna. She's utterly determined to rent the next room she finds tolerable.

The young man conducts her into a small room which is still very bright, the light reaches this far, the sun is shining through the gaps in the cloudbanks. There are no buildings behind casting shadows on the windows, you can see for a long way, and there's even a solitary patch of grass growing down below, so it's the kind of room Erna wants. Here is where she'll stay. All the furniture is very close together, she could probably measure every wall with three strides, but that doesn't matter. Directly underneath the big window there's a broad table which is evidently used as a desk, there are some books lying on it, and magazines and writing paper. Next to them there's a can with a handle, the kind that workers put their lunch in.

'I apologize, all my bits and pieces are still lying around on top of each other. I haven't even got around to making the bed yet. You see, I've had to do everything myself since yesterday, because I had a bust-up with the old cow.'

Erna is surprised, so he's Frau Ziegenbein's lodger. He's got a real boy's face, is wearing a grey wool jersey like the bicycle racers wear, and is looking at her in obvious confusion. And he hasn't shaved, by the way. The pieces of furniture typically found in such rooms are lined up along the walls to the right and left of the door: a cupboard, a dresser, a washstand. Next to them, the boy's clothes are hanging on a hook on the wall. Erna looks at everything closely, and suddenly she realizes that she's staring at that hook, and it has a blue overall jacket on it. Well, that doesn't mean anything! She takes off her beret as she looks around a bit more, she likes the room. The young man is standing behind her, not talking anymore.

'So how much are you paying?'

'Of course, you can ignore me completely if you like', he answers, 'but my advice is not to take it.'

Erna, who's looking out the window, is well aware that he's staring at her. She swings around. He smooths the tablecloth, then puts a few things away, and even pulls up the cover on the bed.

'You see, I've been lodging here until now, which I suppose you've already realized.'

Now he's grinning again, yes, yes, like this morning.

'You wouldn't mind if I lit a cigarette?'

Erna shakes her head.

'Let me tell you something, I'm easy to get on with, but Frau Ziegenbein is unfit for human consumption. We really don't have to put up with the women who let rooms doing what that one thinks she's entitled to do. I'm in favour of just letting the ones like Frau Ziegenbein starve to death. That's why I'm telling you all this, I kind of want to ruin the old girl's business.'

Erna looks at him closely, and she likes him. He has thick, light-coloured hair and a young, cheerful face. She draws her knees together and takes a firm grip on the beret in her lap.

'She wants you to be in bed by nine o'clock at night. You're not allowed to have visitors. You pay for the lighting and the heating in the whole apartment. You can't laugh out loud either. So if you want to put up with all of that and more, you can rent the room.'

'No', Erna says seriously, 'if you've had such bad experiences, I'd rather not take the apartment.'

'Ach, you're sure to find something better.'

'If you knew how long I've been looking today.'

'But there are furnished rooms all over the place.'

'Yes, but they're so expensive. Or they're not nice.'

I suppose I should go now, Erna thinks. It seems odd to her to be sitting in this unfamiliar room and looking out the window as if the neighbourhood interests her.

'I guess you haven't been in Berlin very long?'

'No.'

'Right.'

Hmn. Hmn.

Erna shoots a sideways glance at the boy, she's sure she knows him.

'But you're not from Frankfurt either.'

No, Erna agrees that she's not.

'You see, I worked in construction in Frankfurt for four months, that was a good time, a lot of cash and a nice place to be. There are some bridges over the Main, and the gulls eat out of your hand there, really, out of your hand. Have you ever seen something like that?'

No, Erna hasn't travelled very much, and after they've noted that she says goodbye.

'I could come with you and find something for you, I've got lots of experience with furnished rooms.'

'Well, if you've got so much experience, how come you're renting from Frau Ziegenbein?'

The boy doesn't know how to answer that one. Erna handled that well, and she's pleased. I'll sort you out, young man, she thinks. You were making faces at me this morning, now I've got the last laugh.

The boy looks genuinely unhappy now.

'Nah, I just thought you might like it if I went with you. Just walk on a bit further, you'll see a few nice buildings, you should see if there's anything available there.'

Erna shoots a sideways glance at him and smiles, she puts on her beret, presses his hand in farewell and leaves. His face looks as if he wants to say something. They walk down the passageway, the stairwell lights aren't switched on yet.

'Don't fall down the stairs!'

'I won't … And thanks a lot!'

He leans over the banister and watches as she goes, taking two stairs at a time.

'Are you angry with me, about this morning?'

Her answer comes from down on the first floor, but the little word sounds high and clear in the stairwell.

'No!'

And Erna does find a room after all. Thirty-two marks, and that includes coffee in the morning, which she doesn't think is too expensive.

Down below, the trains bump over an embankment and the smoke rises, licking at the buildings, shrouding the windows.

The room has a bed, a dresser, a small wardrobe. There's a round three-legged table covered by a faded blue cloth with its lace fringes hanging down to the floor. Two chairs. A primitive little washstand with a basin and a jug and a water glass and the usual neatly folded towel, but no soap – what you always find in these furnished rooms.

She doesn't like the woman particularly.

'You'll be comfortable here, would you like to unpack your suitcases now?'

Erna hasn't actually said yet that she wants to rent the room, and Frau Matschek must see that she doesn't have a suitcase with her.

But Erna doesn't leave. For one thing, she likes the view down there, into the jumble of buildings with the gleaming tracks running between them and the trains moving through, and her room is separated from the Matschek family's rooms by a long hallway. She's very pleased about that.

'I'll pay right away.'

Erna blushes as she says this. Frau Matschek goes with slippers flapping and brings the keys. A key to the apartment, one for her room, and one for the street door. She mustn't stick that last one too deeply into the lock, otherwise the door won't open, but she'll soon get the hang of it. When does she want to be woken in the morning?

Then Erna is alone. She sits in the middle of her room and looks around her. Through one wall, she hears plates clattering. One floor down somebody's playing a gramophone, it's hammering out the music. Erna doesn't realize that she's being greeted with 'The Entry of the Guests' from *Tannhäuser*. Down below the trains are whistling, and the echo of the rolling wheels drifts up. A bright sky is swimming past. Berlin, Berlin.

She stands up, washes thoroughly, and examines her face in the mirror. So that's Erna Halbe, not yet nineteen, and alone in the city of Berlin. She feels out of place here. She feels odd and solemn all at the same time.

Would her bob look nicer if it was permed? I can't spend that much money this month, she reflects. She does her accounts. There are thirty-four marks, and in fact thirty-four pfennigs, on the table in front of her. She's got to live for a month on that.

Her landlady knocks. Has she registered her address at the police station yet? No, so she's got to do that as well.

Those little necessary tasks take up the remainder of the afternoon. Registering her address, collecting her suitcase, unpacking her things, arranging the room a bit, buying bread and butter. She walks around and about again through familiar and unfamiliar streets, moving quickly and energetically, there are new things to see everywhere. Now I've got somewhere to live, it's not too bad, she tells herself. And I won't fall flat on my face, I know what I'm doing.

In the evening she wants to see the city, the sea of light and the bustle of the night. She sets off after six. A crisp, clear breeze is still blowing between the buildings, everything is already lit up. The days are getting longer, early, unaccustomed warmth is flowing from the countryside over the city.

She takes the bus, sitting on the open top. It's fun for her to be driven through the evening all by herself, past all the lighted windows, down mysterious streets and across unfamiliar bridges. She takes off her beret, the wind tousles her hair.

She gets out at the quiet Lützow Embankment and strolls slowly into the unfamiliar city. She's breathing calmly, deeply and happily. She's thinking of all kinds of things. I wonder what kind of job the boy from Koppen Street has? You might call that a very interesting question. She has to laugh. Perhaps he's a metalworker. Or even a mechanic.

There's a young girl walking ahead of her, about her age, she's wearing a blue hat with a yellow ribbon at an angle on her head and a light, close-fitting blue silk dress which is so short that Erna can see the backs of her knees. The girl has very slim legs, she's not setting her feet down very firmly, but walking with a bit of a swing, moving lightly and cheerfully without looking around or turning to the side, not paying any attention to the men who turn to look at her. It's fun to follow this chic, elegant girl, who looks so self-confident that Erna envies her. Wouldn't be expensive, a dress like that, she decides. She's daydreaming a bit, and in Genthin Street she almost walks in front of a little yellow car which is making a sharp, tight turn around the corner. Frightened, she stops. The car screeches to a stop too. A bad-tempered, elegant girl who's sitting in it says something very unpleasant to Erna, a lady with a little military-looking hat of white straw and a red-and-blue scarf, with a white-painted face and a remarkably big nose. Erna listens to her with big, wide eyes, and then the car drives off.

The evening and the dark are coming, aureoles of light are starting to shine between the trees, fiery red letters are lining up jerkily along the buildings to form incomprehensible words, the stars drift past above them, and the people below. Strangers look at each other, glances meet, a mouth breathes out a greeting which can't be heard, it disperses, the eye turns away, everybody is walking on, everybody is breathing, feeling and living.

A big cinema poster shows a girl with a clever face and a grey beret, similar to Erna's, skipping up a staircase. There are twenty posters with her doing the same thing, and the arc lamps pick out the garish colours from the darkness of the street. The people are crowding around the box office. Erna hesitates, the cheapest seat costs sixty pfennigs, she finds that very expensive. You can get a private box for that back home. She looks admiringly at the movie theatre's gleaming façade, not realizing that this cinema on the edge of the city, in the middle of a working-class district, is patronized almost entirely by people who work for a living, because Erna is on the other side of Frankfurt Avenue now. In her little coal-mining town you can only go to the movies three days a week, in the main dining room of the biggest restaurant.

'Whaddaya say, little lady, would ya like to be my guest … ? Go on, go on! I'll get us a box in the upper circle …'

The man is following her. Erna runs quickly back into the dark street, she's terribly frightened. The gas lamps hum monotonously, women stand gossiping in the dark open doorways of buildings, there's a little bar jammed in on every corner. The man has stopped, and is now shouting abuse at her.

She returns slowly, crosses the road hurriedly when she reaches the cinema and lines up at the box office.

'One sixty-pfennig ticket.'

The working-class audience, in their Sunday best, are packed into the overcrowded auditorium, the girls are cuddling up to their boys, people are smoking furtively all over the place, the fan is no match for the suffocating atmosphere. Lights of all colours are playing across the ceiling, an excited babble of voices mixes with the music. Erna has to wait quite a while at first, she's standing among a lot of people she doesn't know, but one young man makes room for her. Another one shines a flashlight across the densely occupied rows, and Erna pushes her way through nervously. She bumps into knees and legs and skirts, the people mutter as she moves past, but she finds a seat at last. She's so happy that she closes her eyes for a moment. The program begins solemnly, with the sound of a gong and the boom-boom of the music, first a comedy, then the newsreel, and finally: Kiki. Yes, tonight – her first in Berlin – Erna is watching Kiki, the black-eyed girl with the beret, who is none other than Norma Talmadge. She's a real working-class girl, who has to make her own way and carves out a place for herself. Kiki weeps and Kiki laughs, Kiki as a variety girl and Kiki as a lady. Isn't life wonderful in this cinema? You get to see everything, life out there in the world, life here in the city. Kiki meets a really classy guy, and good luck to her. The fat man sitting next to Erna keeps laughing raucously like an idiot. He's pushed his arm over the seat's arm and is squishing her forcefully. He's making her uncomfortable. When Kiki narrows her eyes or when sometimes she slips up, then he laughs, and lots of men laugh with him. What's there to laugh about? Isn't this a serious, important thing, one that you've got to think about, consider very carefully, would you be as clever as Kiki is? And then the lights go on again, the fat man takes his arm off the seat, everybody gets up, 'Don't miss our coming special program', she feels a bit dizzy, Erna Halbe or Kiki, she goes out, she goes home, her head is buzzing, this evening has taken its toll.

She walks through dim, warm streets, a policeman gives her directions, the streets are becoming emptier and more unfriendly, Erna strides along calmly. She's thinking about her parents, what'll they be doing at home now? I'll have to write to them so that they'll know I've arrived safely, I'm not afraid in this city, they don't need to worry about me …

The street door is open, there's no light burning in the stairwell, this unfamiliar building is dark and disturbing. She walks up slowly, counting the steps and holding on tight to the banister. I'll have to buy a flashlight, she decides. Up above, she doesn't know for sure if she's on the right floor. She gropes around on the door to locate the letterbox, which she had noticed was very low down, and drops her key as she does so.

Once in her room, she switches on the light, opens the window wide and writes a letter to her parents.

> Dear Parents, I've arrived safely, and I've already found a nice place to live too. I'll write my address at the bottom, so that you know where I am. I'm paying 32 marks. With coffee. That isn't very much really, is it? It's just that the prices here are a bit different, and you can't compare it with our little town. The building has five stories, and I've got a proper room all to myself. I like the other things about Berlin too.

> Everything is very big and nice and especially lots of cars. I'll write you more another time. Mother, maybe you can't even imagine how many people there are on the street here, but you don't need to be afraid on my account. How's your leg? I've already been to the cinema too, you could fit our room at the Victoria in there ten times over. The film is called Kiki, you've really got to see it when it gets to the Victoria, it's about a variety girl. I start at my new job tomorrow morning. Cross your fingers for me! That reminds me that Hans should go to see Herr Muschler about that job. I'd forgotten about that. I'm living very high up and now I can see the whole city from my room. I'll write again soon and you should too, so until then
>
> Your Erna.

No, one thing isn't true, she can't see the whole city from her window. The bit in the direction of Frankfurt Avenue, a confusion of buildings with just a few factory chimneys sticking up, wreathed in smoke. Erna is looking directly at the backs of the buildings, the windows are open, she can see the people sitting in their kitchens, around the tables, doing whatever they do every evening. Somebody comes home from a late shift, a railwayman, his wife puts his supper on the table, other people are reading newspapers, listening to the radio, playing, arguing, working. Music comes from the apartment buildings, singing from the cramped courtyards. Accompanied by a melancholy mouth organ, a girl's clear voice sings recent hits interspersed with sad folk songs in which partings and parents' graves play a major role …

For your luh-huv … was untroo-hoo …

At regular intervals, the singing and the music are drowned out by the rumbling of the trains. Jannowitz Bridge Station is on one side, and Silesia Station on the other. The rattling of the wheels echoes for a long time. A clock strikes. Enchanted, wistful world.

Erna takes off her simple, cheap travelling clothes and moves and stretches herself, she's tired, she yawns. Downstairs, the gramophone is playing again. Next door, a man's deep voice is talking forcefully, and the thin walls let through every word, clear and unmistakable: 'I won't have that, I've told you not to, and the next time you and he …'

His next words are less clear, because a girl is crying. Erna listens, and feels ashamed that she's standing at the wall, her heart pounding, eavesdropping on the building's secrets, harnessed to the same journey, to the same fate, sharing walls with people she doesn't know, but whose paths will cross hers. She moves quietly back to the centre of the room and looks at her big, childlike hands, which have already done a lot of heavy work. The short fingers lie straight and close together, their tips have been smoothed a little by typewriting, and the nails are a bit uneven. These fingers are quick to get the job started; they look rather touching. Erna doesn't feel things like that. She knows that she's healthy, and that's enough for her. She brushes her teeth hard with water and salt, then drinks a glass of water, and spits up into the air out of the window, down to the railway embankment or the courtyard or somewhere. The trains are whistling. In the distance she can hear the soothing hum of the city. Erna listens to her heart beating. Then she has a fright, perhaps people in the neighbouring buildings can see her standing here in the electric light, naked and exposed. She moves away from the window and switches off the light cautiously. Her room is very high up, the dark night is drifting by outside, the first lights are shimmering much lower down. She jumps into bed. An unfamiliar, cold, not unpleasant feeling moves up her legs, over her back, to her neck. Breathing heavily, she falls asleep. As she dreams, she tosses from one side to the other, this first day in Berlin won't let go of her.

When Frau Matschek knocks on the door at seven in the morning, she's startled, and sits up and calls out 'Come in!' But she promptly realizes where she is and says quickly: 'Thank you!' Frau Matschek shuffles off slowly.

Erna's a bit embarrassed. She turns over in bed, she can see the sun's warm, yellow light behind the window curtains. The noise is rising from the street, hammering and motors running, she can hear sirens and the rumbling of the subway, the hooting of the trains, Berlin is working.

Directly opposite her window, a bit lower down, next to the big apartment block, a solitary patch of sunlight is shining on the curved, tarred roof of a machinery works which is emitting a peculiar, persistent and penetrating screeching. Erna leans right out of the window and contemplates the patch of sunlight, which looks so pleasantly warm, for a long time. The little courtyards are packed closely together between the expanding, overgrown apartment blocks. A few of them have distinguishing features. One has a rabbit hutch instead of a chicken coop, another has found space somehow for a washing pole which can also be used for beating carpets. Otherwise they're all the same: black, unappealing, embittered. There's some yellow grass growing on the ground raised by the railway. Workshops have been set up in a lot of the ground-floor apartments, the workshops have turned into little businesses, with sheds or annexes added at the back or the side. Higher up, washing is fluttering in many of the windows, with bright red mattresses visible between. The backs of the buildings are bare, grey and windowless, one which faces the railway embankment has been rented to a cosmetics company that has painted a huge shampoo advertisement onto it.

Erna can see the sky too, and that's why it's good to live high up, under the attics, in the big cities. When you're on the street, you forget the sky. It's clear and clean above Berlin, cloudless, smooth, metallic. It smells of grass.

She splashes around in the basin and writes a note on a piece of paper with her still-wet hands: Plain soap.

There's a full-length mirror in the corner next to the washstand, Erna inspects herself in it from the top of her head to the tips of her toes. Her cute little breasts stand out cheekily from her body, pushing upwards slightly. She does a few knee bends, and pulls horrible faces in the mirror. Her feet have grown strong from all her walking without shoes, they look nice and healthy, the toes are a bit widely spread, she jumps up and down happily. The water dries quickly on her skin, she doesn't bother with the towel at all. She runs her slightly-too-big, prominent nose up her white arms to the shoulders. A pleasant aroma of night rest and morning coolness and cold water and clean skin fills her nostrils. A clock strikes again, I wonder what time it is?

A man crosses the courtyard down below. She can hear somebody beating carpets. Radio speakers are chirping from lots of the windows, with a variety of sounds, as if every set is tuned to a different station.

Frau Matschek knocks. The coffee! The old woman looks as if she slept badly and hasn't washed, her hair is hanging down over her forehead, she launches into a lengthy apology.

When the landlady leaves at last, Erna breathes out. She fishes the company's letter out of her suitcase again.

Wednesday morning, nine o'clock, Prenzlau Avenue.

She enquires of Frau Matschek where that is and then sets off, for the first time, to work. No, that should be to the office, Erna Halbe decides.

Before she leaves her room, she stands in front of the mirror again and examines herself very carefully, from top to bottom. A feverish impatience has grabbed hold of her.

Of course, she gets there much too early. She looks at it carefully from outside, a two-story building which looks like a grand house, with a big wrought-iron gate and a black sign which says 'Iron Processing Co.' in gold letters.

The main entrance is through a depressed-looking front garden, the other one goes around the side to the back. That's for the employees, and takes you along a yellow gravel path past a car garage, through a big gate and into a white-painted and apparently newly erected building at the side.

So that's where I'm supposed to work.

She stands still and looks up at the big clock over the entrance. She's already had quite a few jobs and knows very well that you don't get anything as a gift, she's clear-eyed and without illusions, but still she's trembling a little as she stands by herself outside this big building where she's now going to be working eight hours a day for a hundred and thirty marks a month. She's still expecting a great deal from life and has hope in her heart, there are many roads which lead to happiness, and maybe one of them passes through this building. This is her first job in Berlin, she'll turn nineteen here, what will the days and weeks and months bring for her, she doesn't know, she has no inkling, nobody can tell her that, she's trembling a little.

At ten minutes to nine Erna Halbe walks up past rooms and counters, following the little arrow: Visitors Report to Administration.

There's nothing to distinguish this building from other office buildings, but the corridors are empty, there's nobody to be seen.

Behind her a door is open, she can hear voices. A girl comes running out of a room and almost bumps into Erna.

'Trude has fainted again ... Oh!' This last exclamation is one of surprise, when the girl sees that she's speaking to a stranger. She runs on quickly, and disappears into another room.

Trude? Erna doesn't know any Trude.

She can see into the room the girl came from. Another, white-faced girl is sitting on a chair with her eyes closed. Four or five young girls are standing around her.

'Get my smelling salts from my handbag, quick!'

'No, we'd better phone for a doctor.'

'Ach, she usually feels better quite soon.'

Erna is curious, and steps closer. The girls aren't doing much. One is holding the unconscious woman's head, to no purpose.

'The correct thing to do is rub the young lady's face with cold water!' she says.

They look at her in astonishment.

'Well, is that any use?'

'Quick! Cold water!'

Two girls run out.

'And open a window! The air's bad here.'

'Yes', says a little red-cheeked girl who's standing next to Erna and smiling at her, 'I already said that.'

She unhooks the unconscious girl's collar and unbuttons her blouse a little, revealing a clean lace camisole. The office girls look closely at the stranger who is taking charge so resolutely. One of them hands her a glass of water, Erna splashes it into the pale, beautiful face. The drops roll slowly over the big, full lips, collect in the deep dimple between the lower lip and the strong chin, and then fall past the neck.

Behind her, the girls are muttering and whispering. Then a masculine voice speaks.

'Carry Fräulein Leussner to my office!'

But Fräulein Leussner is just coming to. Erna looks into sky-blue and surprisingly lively eyes which are staring blankly at her.

'Water', the girl says, and drinks.

Her white mouth presses firmly onto the glass, which Erna has to hold because the girl's slim hands are fluttering weakly in the air. One finger has a ring with a shiny blue stone.

'Well, Fräulein Trude, are you feeling well again?'

That's the gentleman to whose office Fräulein Leussner was to have been carried. His clean-shaven, somewhat puffy face, with a scar on one cheek, appears next to Erna. He has thin, neatly parted hair, his suit sits well on him, he has a worried expression. Erna is surprised that Trude Leussner doesn't answer, or even look at him.

'Well, children, back to work!' He throws out his hands, as if he's trying to drive a flock of geese back into their yard. He looks at Erna in astonishment. She hasn't taken off her coat yet, her beret is askew, her cheeks are glowing with excitement.

The girls leave, only an elegant, long-legged being and the red-cheeked one stay to look after Trude and talk to her.

'Does it hurt anywhere?' the little one asks.

'No, let me rest a bit.'

'But you must go home', Erna says.

Three very surprised faces turn to her.

'What do you mean, go home?' the tall girl asks, 'you can see that Fräulein Leussner is already feeling better.'

Erna doesn't quite know what to answer. And the pale girl waves her hand deprecatingly. There's an embarrassed silence. Erna feels that she has to explain the reason why she's appeared so suddenly in this room.

'I've been engaged here.'

What a silly thing to say: engaged! She corrects herself promptly.

'What I mean is, I'm starting as a typist here.' And she takes the letter from Iron Processing Co. out of her handbag.

'Right! You're the new girl. From Merseburg, aren't you?'

'No.'

The little red-cheeked girl is beaming, two deep little dimples on her plump cheeks are shining.

'Hello, I'm Lotte Weissbach.'

She holds out a small hand, Erna shakes it warmly.

'So you can take her details.' Then the elegant, somewhat arrogant being leaves. Erna watches her admiringly. She's particularly impressed by the beautiful long legs, and the openwork shoes on the small feet and a wonderful black-and-white checked suit.

Lotte Weissbach looks at Erna and jerks her thumb at the door.

'That's Erika Tümmler. And she has a big say here. Well, we'd better go to the back, to my room. You see, I've got an office to myself.'

The sick girl, Trude, stays sitting comfortably in her chair, she's using a pocket mirror to tidy her beautiful ash-blonde hair.

They walk down a long corridor, with Lotte leading the way. The other girls are nowhere to be seen, but behind one door lots of typewriters are hammering away, the little incident mustn't disrupt the work.

ADMINISTRATION. Enter Without Knocking.

The sunlight flows in a strong, broad stream through big, open sliding windows into the little room, which is at the back of the building. Beyond it, a garden sets this building apart from the other blocks, obscuring the view in a most pleasant way with shifting waves of branches and twigs. Lotte drops into a chair and looks at Erna with her protuberant eyes; she's a nice girl, looks like Clara Bow, Erna decides, she knows all about Clara Bow. Lotte's thick, soft brown hair falls gracefully over her forehead in a fringe. Her cheerful eyes aren't afraid of anybody, least of all this shy new girl from the provinces.

'Wow, the way you helped Trude, I was impressed. Like a proper nurse, Fräulein Halbe!'

Erna has to laugh.

'But you learn that at school. If somebody faints, fresh air and splash water and all that.'

'Nah, we didn't learn that. Actually, it happens to Trude a lot, it didn't before, but for the last few weeks she's been fainting all the time, I don't know what's up with the girl. I don't suppose you like Erika much, do you?'

Erika? Erna pretends not to understand.

'Yes, Fräulein Erika Tümmler. The tall one with the checked suit. She's got a big say here, she can stick her neck out now and then. She's Siodmak's secretary, and Siodmak's the big cheese around here. As to Lortzing, the one who was just in the room, he's all hot air, you got it? A big mouth with nothing to back it up …'

Erna listens in astonishment. She can learn stuff here. She's got to have at least a vague idea of what the bosses are like and how you should behave. This little one is certain to give her good information. She pays attention, trying to take note of what the girl is telling her.

But the room is warm, Erna's head is fuzzy, she can't listen properly, her eyes are hurting, typewriters are clacking in other rooms, it sounds like bees buzzing, she's getting tired, so tired …

'Oh well, you'll soon get the hang of how we do things, Fräulein Halbe.'

The little girl's round eyes are laughing. She has a curiously deep voice.

'We've all got to stick together a bit, don't we? I was impressed by how decisively you did it, the thing with Trude. Oh yeah, what I need first is your tax card, Erna.'

While she's speaking, she touches up her lipstick without looking in a mirror.

'We take care of the whole deal for everybody, health insurance and unemployment insurance and tax, I do all that. I suppose you don't have a problem with the local health insurer, Fräulein Halbe?

The telephone rings, she puts the call through.

'Have you got somewhere to live already, Erna … ?'

Erna doesn't say much at all, and when she does say something, she takes great care to avoid addressing Lotte directly, because what's she supposed to say when the little girl keeps jumping around between 'Fräulein Halbe' and 'Erna'?

'It's my first time in Berlin, this is only my third job, and I can type really fast.'

'Touch-typing? Good, you've got nothing to worry about. So I'll look after you a bit, Erna. I know what it's like, being alone like that. You'll like the other girls in the company here well enough, some of them are a bit pleased with themselves. There's no need to get upset if they say something now and again, they don't really mean it. You're all together in one room. Except for me. And Erika Tümmler, she works with Siodmak. Now, what did I want from you, Erna? Oh yes, your tax card …'

She types up what Erna tells her right away, her rather thick fingers skipping quickly over the keys. She has firm, well-formed hands, although they're a bit small and broad.

Erna leans forward onto the desk and watches closely. The little girl talks a bit too freely, she decides, but of course she's only saying what she really thinks. Erna likes her.

'You don't need to worry about Trude Leussner. Today wasn't the first time, she often – What did you say? Anaemic? No, no, she's got a screw loose somewhere.'

She has to sign, that's the end of the formalities, Erna Halbe is now officially an employee of Iron Processing Co., Berlin, Prenzlau Avenue, one hundred and thirty marks per month. Lotte grins happily, puts her arm through Erna's, and they leave the office.

The long corridor again, and at the end there's a room, you can hear the typewriters hammering away behind the door. Everything goes quiet when Lotte and Erna walk in, everybody looks up. They look carefully at the new girl, the way she's dressed, the way she stands, face, legs and hair-style. Erna is still wearing her inadequate coat, and underneath it a simple everyday blouse and the dark blue skirt, her red hair is sticking out from under her beret. She stands with her legs pressed together, gathers her courage and says loudly: 'Good morning!'

The girls answer.

'This is Erna Halbe', Lotte trills, 'behave yourselves!'

'We will obey, Queen of the Tax Cards!' a funny girl answers.

Erna laughs with the cheeky one, who's sitting close to the door, and all the others laugh too.

The girl rocks back and forth on her chair, looks at Erna and says: 'You see, Lotte sometimes gets a bit too big for her boots, so she needs a rap over her inky knuckles, you'll need to remember that!'

She jumps onto her chair, draws up her legs comfortably and looks at Erna carefully. Her name is Elsbeth Siewertz, and she isn't what you'd call pretty, Erna decides. No, definitely not. So what is she? A bit simple? Or cunning behind it, more likely? But it's no less than rude to be looking at Erna so intently. Still, the girl has clever, warm eyes which miss nothing as they dart around observing everything attentively. Elsbeth's hair is combed resolutely upwards from a parting on the right, and it's a flaming red. The reason she's no beauty is probably because all her features, nose, mouth, ears, forehead and chin, are out of proportion with each other. One is too big, another too small, the third too thick. It takes a while for Erna to realize all that, and then she has to look at something else for a change. And Elsbeth Siewertz's remark about Lotte was meant as a harmless joke, Erna sees that immediately, and Lotte is laughing about it too.

The room is bare, functional and rather cramped, the top sections of the walls are painted blue. The girls are sitting in two long rows, all facing the same way, all the same distance from each other. Some of the seats are vacant.

'Well, Erna', Lotte says, 'two of the typewriters are being repaired at the moment. You'll have to sit at that rattly Orga Privat for a while.'

Aha! The new girl is already being called by her first name! The girls look at each other, pulling faces. That's going pretty fast. Usually it takes a long time before a new girl settles in and enjoys the privileges the others do. Either Lotte has got a bee in her bonnet or she's really that stupid or …

What are you supposed to say to this little country mouse?

Elsbeth Siewertz leans across to a plump little blonde: 'Hey, look at that blouse!'

Because Erna has taken off her coat and her beret and put everything in the girls' cloakroom, which is in a little alcove.

She's well aware of how they're staring at her, that's not very pleasant, she's a stranger among these girls, she's alone. Yes, of course, Lotte is sticking up for her, it won't be as hard as all that, but she knows that she'll blush again when Elsbeth looks in her direction. The girls have got pretty things, nice clothes, there are nine girls, Erna has already counted. Some of them, including Elsbeth, are still looking at her, the others are typing again.

Erna tries out her Orga Privat, it's a heavy, rattly machine. It makes a grinding noise like a coffee mill.

The other girls are typing on nice new machines.

'Oh well, doesn't matter', Erna says.

'Fine, then you'll work at this desk.'

'What should I do to begin with?'

'Not so fast! We're going to see Siodmak first.'

Erna sees how all the girls look up at once, one even laughs. She has an odd laugh, soft and gurgling.

Erna walks behind Lotte as far as the door, where she stops, because Elsbeth is waving to her.

'Hey, listen!'

Elsbeth twists her mouth as she speaks, it's startlingly red, Elsbeth uses a lot of makeup. Her father is a driver on the subway, so she comes from a humble background. Her girlfriends still haven't worked out where she gets her nice clothes and movie tickets from all the time. All they know is that Elsbeth has the smartest mouth in the whole office, and that she doesn't put up with anything from Lortzing or even Siodmak. She's not pretty, there's nothing silly about her face and, surprisingly, she hasn't gone to the bad or got carried away, she's walking straight ahead through her young life and knows exactly what she wants. She looks calmly at Erna, smiling with her pulled-down mouth.

'Enjoy yourself!'

'Thanks very much!'

'Make sure you come back in one piece.'

The girls laugh again, with speaking faces. Only Lotte taps Elsbeth on the forehead.

'You! You're meschugge!' And she says to Erna: 'Come on! Let them talk their nonsense.'

As they're leaving the room, Trude Leussner comes back in.

'Well, Trude, what do you think of our latest acquisition?'

'Was that the new girl?'

'Of course it was.'

'Iron Processing Co.'s diva.'

'So what's her name?'

Yes, Lotte had mentioned the name, what is it again? Nobody can say, they've forgotten it.

'So let's just call her "The Lil' Girl at the Orga Privat"!' Elsbeth suggests.

Yes, it's really interesting that one of them is to use that clapped-out old thing.

'She must be stupid', a heavily made-up girl says.

'Who's stupid?' Elsbeth spins around like lightning on her chair, her legs dangling in the air. 'I suppose you're all upset because you didn't get another little doll-like one, are you? Anybody who says anything to that little girl about her clothes will have me to deal with, got it?'

The typewriters rattle away.

Meanwhile, The Girl at the Orga Privat is walking down the long corridor to be introduced to Director Siodmak, who always wishes to see the new employees. As this department of Iron Processing Co. consists mainly of stenotypists, there's no doubt about why.

Lotte disappears to report Erna's arrival.

The only other occupant of the little anteroom is a fly, emitting a low-pitched buzz as it endlessly circles the walls, which are also ringed with industrial photos, all hung at the same height in simple black frames. Blast furnaces, machines, cranes. Otherwise it's quiet, you can't even hear the typewriters here, and when Erna turns around her shoe squeaks alarmingly loudly.

But Lotte comes straight back and motions her towards the door.

'I'll wait here.'

Erna isn't nervous anymore now, she opens the door calmly and walks into the director's room. She sees a few club chairs and a big desk with cigar smoke drifting across it. There's nothing else to be seen, no director, nothing, she's alone.

She stands there, unruffled, and examines the room a bit more closely. A lovely smooth washbasin has been let into the wall next to the door. A long bookcase with lots of books … Erna turns around, startled, something is scraping and rustling behind her. From behind the bookcase, which divides the room into two in an extremely clever way, a suit jacket appears which is framed at one end by a gleaming bald head and extends at the other end into two short legs. As Erna assumes that this suit jacket could be hiding only Director Siodmak, she offers him a vigorous 'Good morning' the instant her initial surprise has passed.

And then they look at each other for a moment.

The director smiles with his smooth, rosy baby's face, rubs his hands jovially and advances a few paces. He inspects Erna from top to bottom, rubs his right hand over his chin, and finally contemplates the tips of his shoes intently.

'Your name, Fräulein?'

'Erna Halbe.'

'Fräulein Tümmler should be able to explain everything to you. Hm! You're from Berlin?' As he asks, he looks up.

'No.'

'One can see that, one can see that. Do you already have somewhere to live?'

'Yes.'

'I see.'

He puts his hands behind his back and wanders back and forth in the room. Erna feels quite comfortable.

'How old are you?'

'Nineteen next birthday.'

'I see. You'll need to be a bit careful in Berlin, won't you? The thing about young girls is … They never know what's the right thing and who's the right person, do you know what I mean?'

'Yes.'

'And you must do your work well and carefully.'

'Yes.'

He turns away, extending his left hand casually as he does so. When Erna shakes it, she feels how damp it is.

Then the little girl goes out again.

'Well', Lotte asks, 'how did it go?'

'It was good.'

'Well then, everything's alright.'

Lotte doesn't say anything more on the subject, and Erna doesn't ask either. When she gets back to the typists' room Lortzing is there, and all the girls are bent industriously over their work. Nobody looks up.

Erna is given a file for copying, a complicated, technical, special explanation. She tries hard to type quickly and cleanly and to avoid any mistakes.

The girls are sitting in rows, like in school. Each one has a little desk with the typewriter on the right-hand side, leaving a narrow margin on the left where she can put down copies, files and other papers. Every desk has a little drawer where the girls store their bits and pieces, mostly sandwiches, mirrors, combs, powder compacts, lipsticks, hairpins, books, magazines, letters and things like that, all mixed up together.

Even when Lortzing disappears, the girls remain silent for a while. They have to get used to the stranger, who's sitting there a bit lonely and isolated among all their friendships and confidences.

Erna furtively examines their short hairstyles: bobbed, permed, curled somewhere or everywhere, combed out. All the girls are already wearing bright, airy dresses, the first hint of summer is already blossoming in their young hearts. Compared to them, Erna finds her everyday blouse rather inadequate.

The girl directly in front of her is Trude Leussner, typing quickly and accurately. You can't tell that an hour ago she was slumped unconscious and helpless on the floor. Incidentally, she's the only girl who's still wearing plaits, long, light-coloured plaits. Lotte and Erika are working in other rooms, but Elsbeth Siewertz is looking in her direction again. The cheeky girl is laughing. Erna smiles too. The typewriters are pounding away, the papers are rustling, outside the sun is shining. Mild, gentle morning warmth fills the room.

A slim, nondescript girl starts whistling, sticking her lips out oddly and striking the keys of her typewriter in time with the music. First she tries 'What Are You Doing With Your Knee, Hans Dear?', following it up promptly with another hit. She knows lots of popular songs, it sounds nice, it helps you to type, and the whistling girl is obviously proud of herself, because now and then she shoots a sideways glance through the room to see if everybody is listening. And she has good reason to be proud, because everybody is enjoying it. Erna calls out another popular title, and she tries that one too. The girl's name is Friedel. While she whistles, the others type on without interruption.

After a while Friedel stops, she's getting tired. A conversation moves from desk to desk, one girl has something to say, then another does. They talk about men and about dancing, they talk about cinemas and about clothes, but the typewriters don't hesitate for a moment. Erna listens. She doesn't say anything herself, but she listens carefully. She wonders how old the girls are, older or younger or the same age as Erna, what will she learn from them, what kinds of things will she learn and experience here, in this city of Berlin?

A morning like this passes slowly, the girls look at their wristwatches, comparing the different times and arguing about minutes. They count the quarter-hours. On the dot of one o'clock, they all put on their coats and disappear.

'How much time do we have for lunch?'

'Two hours', a little girl with a serious face answers.

The little girl enquires where Erna is going to eat. But then Lotte Weissbach comes in, and stands next to her.

'Come and eat with us, Erna.'

'Where?'

'Come on, I know you'll like it.'

Erna thinks of her thirty marks. What should she do? She can't have lunch in a restaurant every day on thirty marks. But she can't tell the girls that she has so little money either, she's rather ashamed. Well, she'll go this one time, she can find some excuse to duck out other times.

The little serious girl joins them, she doesn't say much. Her face reminds Erna of somebody, she doesn't know who, anyway it's not a very memorable face, very thin and with an unhealthy skin colour. And her dress is also remarkably different from what the other stenotypists are wearing, Erna is astonished that she's only noticed it now. The grey material makes the little one look very mousy, over it she's wearing a brown off-the-rack coat similar to our Erna's one.

The three girls go to a kind of dining hall behind Alexander Square, where you eat on a ticket system. There's a handwritten sign stuck on the thick glass outside:

Lunch for 60, 80 and 100 Pfennigs.

Otherwise there's nothing to show what kind of business it is. No drinks are served, just mineral water and lately, at the request of the young girls who come here, milk as well. And this is where the young people from the shops and offices around Alexander Square come to meet. Boys who live a long way from their place of work and don't want to go home for lunch; girls who are lodging alone in rooms and can't afford to cook for themselves. They can't spend much on food, after all, they receive a pittance for the eight and nine and even longer hours they sit in their offices. But they're all cheerful, well, not always, but they have bright, clear faces and have a firm grip on their little lives. This little dining hall is a story in itself. New words, new heroes and many new problems have appeared, it's the year 1928, we must help each other as friends, sometimes because it's the only thing we can do.

Most of the guests have multitickets, because that reduces the prices to fifty-five, seventy-five and ninety-five pfennigs.

Lotte eats in first class.

'Listen, the multitickets are much cheaper! And it tastes really good, so there's nothing to complain about, right, Martha?'

Oh well, Erna thinks, I've got to eat something, there's no help for it, she buys a ticket for ten of the cheapest meals.

'Wow! You'll still be hungry!'

'Got to save', Erna says.

Lotte is served potato soup first, then a grilled sausage with potatoes, a bit of sauce and some salad. Erna only gets the sausage and potatoes. The quiet girl whom Lotte addresses as Martha orders an extra serving of pea soup.

'I suppose you haven't met yet? This is Martha Hummel, Elfriede Hummel's sister, married and divorced again, and this is Erna Halbe. Right, you can eat now.'

Erna eats, and looks across the table. The young girl is supposed to be divorced, but she looks like a child.

'You'll get to know all the girls at Iron Processing Co. soon enough. Only two of them are married, Eva Hagedorn and Lieselotte Kries. I'll point them out to you in the office sometime. How old? Wait a moment. Eva is nineteen, isn't she? She's only staying with us for a few more months, then she'll be running her own household. And Lieselotte's twenty-two or so. Erika is the oldest, Erika Tümmler, the one who said her little bit to you. Yes, she's twenty-six, currently Siodmak's right hand in business and love. Get it? You'll learn. Tell me, how much are you paying where you live?'

At the next table, a traveller in cosmetics is explaining that this is his first hot lunch in three weeks, and he doesn't know how he'll get on tomorrow. Lotte leans around and asks if he carries Khasana. He says No, but he has another excellent face powder … Then his case is on the table. The girls look at the samples eagerly. Some come over from other tables and join the conversation. A pimple-faced youth smelling of scent wants to tell a couple of 'really excellent' jokes, but nobody pays any attention to him.

'Get lost, you', a little girl tells him. Her face is a picture of outrage, and the youth turns away, offended. Erna talks with Martha Hummel, who remains serious and taciturn beyond her years. Erna tells her what she did before now, what jobs she had, and what it was like at home.

Lotte can't make up her mind, and Martha can't help her. A girl at another table calls out something to her. Everybody seems to know everybody else here, the conversations shift from table to table, nobody needs to introduce themselves, the young people all belong together. There's a loose camaraderie, a camaraderie for the lunchbreak, but that's much nicer than reserve. And really they all know each other: They eat here every day, their lunchbreaks are almost at the same time, they see each other in the streets around Alexander Square, they know where this boy works and that girl. That creates a camaraderie which is strengthened further by their similarity in age. For example, Martha explains to the attentive Erna Halbe that the tall, broad-shouldered boy over there with the face of a friendly dog is a sales assistant in a bookshop. He has to set up the displays every Saturday, and people say that they all collapse. Of course, she's never seen it herself, but that's the story the girls tell. The two sisters over there with yellow perms are qualified hairdressers. They want to set up their own salon someday, and they've been saving for ages.

The owner, a jovial man with a thick red moustache who contributes one or two sentences to the conversations everywhere, serves the food himself. He's wearing a simple coat, and looks more like a guest.

Erna looks around. Almost all the tables are occupied. There's a big green sofa against the wall, a few girls are sitting on it. One is sobbing quietly to herself, and the others are trying to comfort her. What's going on with her? Lotte goes over and talks to the girl. They know each other, they tell each other their problems, they help where they can.

'She's a typist in an oil company. Her branch is being wound up, and twenty employees will be on the street. A bad thing for the girl, alone in Berlin, no parents. She'll starve on the little bit of unemployment assistance she'll get.'

A tall, slim girl with startlingly thick red hair gets up from the next table and goes over to the sofa.

'Yes, Hilde, you look after her!'

'Stop crying! We'll help you look for something. If you see something in the paper, apply for it. Yes, yes, I know … You're not stupid … Tell me, didn't you have a boyfriend?'

The boys and girls at the tables are listening closely.

'Fritz is unemployed too.'

'Well, don't worry, you're sure to find something.'

The little girl stops crying, she only sniffles softly to herself and gives a deep, dry sob now and then.

'So, Hilde', a boy says to the red-headed girl, 'you thought she needed a different boyfriend, did you? If Fritz was here, he'd beat you to a pulp.'

The red-headed girl doesn't say a thing, she just smiles at the boy, and Erna notices how her brown eyes are shining.

But another girl answers.

'I'd look for a boyfriend, sooner than starving to death.'

'And what would you all do if you couldn't snare rich boyfriends, hey?' The traveller in cosmetics is speaking very sharply from two tables away. 'You say that without thinking, in passing, when it's alright again. But what about beforehand, hey? There aren't nearly enough half-way affluent men living in Berlin to take care of all the nice unemployed girls. If none of you knows any other way out ...'

The red-headed girl is still smiling.

'You men aren't supposed to do anything. Does anybody think I'm so stupid as to tell the kid, do hmn-hmn-hmn, that'll solve the whole mess? You're all nuts. I only wanted to find out if she's on her own or not.'

'Then what?'

'What do you mean: Then what? That's entirely up to her Fritz. I don't know him at all.'

The little girl chips in again, Fritz would help her sure enough, but if he doesn't have anything himself, he can't give anything.

The radio is playing the midday program.

Lotte turns back round to Erna, she counts up which girls in the office are living in rooms, and which ones with their parents. From this Erna learns that Friedel with all the hit songs is Martha's sister. Friedel is just the name people call her by, her proper name is Elfriede Hummel. Now Erna also understands why Martha had reminded her of somebody. Of course, she looks like the little whistling girl.

A total of thirteen girls, including Erna, are employed in the company's typing pool. Lotte, Elsbeth, the two Hummel sisters, an Ottilie Heynicke (Otti for short), whom she hasn't met yet, and of course Erna herself are living in rooms. The two married girls, Lieselotte Kries and Eva Hagedorn (the plump little blonde who looked Erna over) have their own apartments, and the remaining five girls are still living with their parents.

Erna eats slowly, chewing every single bite thoroughly and hoping that this will make her feel less hungry. The tables are covered with paper. There aren't any napkins. You get through the food damned quickly, every bite is precious, the sausage is getting smaller and smaller and Erna's appetite is getting bigger and bigger. But she's got to conquer that appetite and all the temptations that go with it, otherwise she'll run out of money.

After the meal some guests read, the boys talk about football and boxing matches, the girls about restaurants on the river Havel where the dancing is good, because spring is coming, bringing the sun with it. New movies and the price of clothes are popular topics too.

A few young men are sitting idly around, smoking slowly and watching the smoke drift away.

Erna sits by herself, listening to the radio. Then she fetches some magazines, well-thumbed old issues, and dozes over them. Lotte and Martha have moved their chairs together and are whispering about something or other. It must be an important conversation, Lotte's face is heated, and Martha's is thoughtful. You might think that Lotte was remonstrating with the pale girl.

Erna turns her eyes to her magazines, she doesn't want to eavesdrop. She only picks up some words when Lotte becomes even more heated.

'That won't work,' Lotte is saying, 'he'll fetch the police, and that'll be the end of you.'

'But what else can I do, I've been thinking about it from every angle.'

'Did you go there again?'

'Of course, he's got a nanny, I told you. He doesn't really care, but I can't go on like this.'

Erna starts to read the serial in a magazine in the middle somewhere, she reads a few lines which don't have any context, things which don't interest her, fates which barely touch her, she doesn't know where they begin or end. The red-headed girl who helped the little typist from the oil company walks past her table and out the door on her beautiful long legs, treading slowly, deliberately, but very softly, you can't hear her walking, you only feel it, a gentle, cat-like tread. All you notice are the strong joints and the slim ankles. Sometimes you're frightened that she'll fall out of her little shoes. From a distance, she seems to walk with a swing. Erna follows her with her eyes admiringly. After the girl has gone, the traveller in cosmetics remarks to a middle-aged gentleman who looks like he's ended up in the dining hall by mistake: 'Look at that, the girl walks like Greta Garbo.' The middle-aged gentleman doesn't understand.

The two hours pass quickly. They leave. The two young women are still talking about the same thing, about a man. Lotte is abusing him, saying that he's a vulgar creep, she could sort him out alright, and Martha would be an idiot to waste any more time worrying about him.

Are they talking about Martha Hummel's former husband? Erna wonders. And Martha's voice can be surprisingly vigorous.

'But what can they do to me?' she asks.

'No, let's leave it now.'

Lotte shoots a sideways glance at Erna, who's not paying any more attention to the conversation. She's looking at the shop windows. A little later, Lotte puts her arm through hers again.

Just before they reach the office, they run into Lieselotte Kries. Lieselotte is one of the married girls, a warm-blooded, affectionate creature. She's wearing a new hat, a cap of blue material with a silver clip.

'From my Manni! I've just dragged him into town with me. Charming, isn't it?'

Lotte wants to try it on, there in the street.

'Cute! I've been wanting a new soft felt one for ages.'

Lieselotte makes friends with everybody immediately, in a few short minutes she asks Erna much more than Lotte and Martha did in the whole lunchbreak between them, she wants to know where Erna comes from and how old she is, if she likes to go out dancing and if she's ever been in Berlin before ... She puts her arm through Erna's too.

'Nice, isn't it, to have a husband who buys you a hat, just like that; if I think I'll like something then I want to have it.'

'Do you want to keep coming to the office, as a married woman?' Erna asks.

'Oh, you silly little thing!' You can smell Lieselotte's perfume as, with a superior expression, she laughs. 'Do you think my husband earns enough for two? He's a bookkeeper, six years older than me. He does what he enjoys, and I do what I enjoy. He's really a good guy, a lovely guy, we get on brilliantly. He gives me enough money too, yes, but if I didn't have my hundred and fifty marks as well, then there'd be lots of things I couldn't buy. Neither of us gets in the other's way, and you should take note of that, it always pays off!'

Yes, Erna does take note of that the same afternoon, in a rather odd and, as she thought, shameful way. Because Lotte had told her that she should take the copies which she finished to Herr von Lortzing, the pudgy gentleman with the conspicuous scar who had come into the room that morning when Trude Leussner was lying there in a faint. Lotte had also shown her where Lortzing's room was.

But Erna forgot. She had a lot to do, the papers were piling up next to her, she was being particularly industrious, and she stopped thinking about Herr von Lortzing. Suddenly Elsbeth Siewertz prods her in the back. Erna looks up.

'Hey, you've still got all your carbon copies sitting there.'

'Oh dear! I forgot! What should I do?'

'Hurry over there, quick!'

So Erna gathers her papers together and rushes down the corridor, but Lortzing's door is locked. What should she do? There's another room on the right, she saw her boss disappearing into it that morning, and Lotte explained to her that it was his private sanctum. But unfortunately Lotte forgot to tell her that all employees are forbidden to enter that room, so Erna just opens the door without thinking anything of it, moving quickly in her anxiety to be rid of the papers she should have brought before.

She sees Lortzing sitting in a deep armchair directly opposite the door, with a cigar, the smoke is drifting through the room, there's a smell of perfume too. Her first fleeting glance also shows her how small and elegant the room is.

Lortzing is sitting there. Erna stands stock-still for a moment, then she dumps the papers on the desk and rushes out, runs to the typists' room and starts hammering out some job or other on her typewriter, just so that she's doing something to help her get over the shock of what she's just seen. Herr von Lortzing was sitting in his armchair, and on his lap, hugging him closely as if she was trying to hide from Erna somehow, sat Lieselotte Kries. One strap of her dress had slipped down over her bare arm, Erna can still see the plump round breast, white and lascivious, spilling out of her bodice.

The telephone in the room rings.

Trude Leussner looks over to Erna.

'You're wanted in Herr von Lortzing's office again.'

Erna walks back, her heart pounding.

Lortzing is still sitting in the same place, Lieselotte has disappeared.

'What did you think you were doing, slamming the carbons onto the desk and rushing out without a word? Where did you learn manners like that, hey?'

He stands, and walks up and down with short, vigorous strides, Lotte told her that Lortzing used to be an army officer.

'How long have you been here?'

'I started today.'

'I mean here in Berlin?'

'Only today.' Actually, yesterday, she thinks.

'I see.'

He stands still, and examines her from top to bottom. He examines her slowly and intently, and Erna's eyes narrow sharply, because she's really angry. His thick tongue appears, flickers out and disappears again.

'Your age?'

'I'm turning nineteen in August.'

She's surprised that she can still talk so calmly.

'I suppose you don't have a boyfriend yet?'

Erna bites her teeth together, her cheeks flame red, she's trembling, she has tears in her eyes, it's pure anger. She'd like to spit in the man's face.

But he smiles as he looks at her and draws on his cigar.

'Well, I'll overlook it just this once.'

He waves his cigar at the door, and she leaves. What'll he overlook, hey? Which of them was unpleasant, disgusting, dirty?

He calls her back.

'Oh, yes … You didn't see anything, of course! I think we understand each other.'

Erna walks slowly back to the typists' room. She presses her lips together firmly. Lieselotte is sitting in her chair again, she's typing industriously. Just for a moment, she looks over to Erna, just for a little moment, then she continues typing. Her beautiful brown hair is sticking up in the air.

The day wears on.

'Hey, hey ... you, you ... Fräulein at the Orga Privat!' Eva Hagedorn, the plump little married one, calls out. 'Tell me, where did you buy that blouse?'

'I made it myself.'

'It keeps you warm, does it?'

All the girls can see that Erna's unfashionable and not very pretty blouse is much too warm for this time of year, and is also a bit too small for her. So Eva Hagedorn is being nasty, they all know that, and Erna knows it too. She wants to wear the blouse for a while longer, a new one will cost money which she doesn't have.

'I can make myself wristbands out of it later.'

The girls laugh.

'Would you all stop your stupid teasing!'

Erna looks over in surprise at Martha Hummel, who's speaking to the other girls for the first time that day. She has a forceful voice, nobody challenges her. She's short and thin, her hair is neatly parted, she's sitting separately from the other girls next to the window, her hands are on her typewriter, and she's looking angrily across at Eva Hagedorn.

'Eva, you're already so secure in your marriage that you've completely forgotten how a single girl has to fight to get by. Do you know how much a new blouse costs?'

'God, when any of you has no money, you just have to find yourself an admirer. Don't pretend.'

Elsbeth sits down on her little desk and peels herself an orange. She flicks a bit of the peel in Eva's direction and says quite calmly: 'You all just stop your nonsense right now.'

Erna listens intently, crouching slightly with little, narrowed eyes. That's the second conversation in one day about the topic which interests everybody and is apparently inexhaustible: the minimum they can live on, marriage, boyfriends.

The typewriters rattle away, a gentle late-afternoon breeze with a storm brewing behind it wafts by outside, across the roofs of Berlin, and the girls are chattering in among it all. Erna doesn't say anything, she just listens, she learns things, measures them against what she knows, ponders them. She observes her fellow workers carefully, takes note of their words, and thinks long and hard about them. Suddenly somebody taps her on the shoulder. She turns around. Lieselotte! Erna is quite frightened at first. Why? She doesn't know, and she can't explain it to herself either.

'Can I walk with you for a bit this evening?'

'Yes, I'd like that, but I've already promised Lotte Weissbach ...'

'Then tomorrow for sure, alright?'

Lieselotte presses her hand, looks down at her with big, innocent eyes and disappears again.

Erna is still blushing. What she said about Lotte was an excuse, of course, she hasn't got anything planned for this evening at all. Is she afraid of this Lieselotte? But whatever for? Or maybe she's just afraid of what this twenty-two-year-old married woman will say. Lieselotte is sure to tell her a long story in which she'll be an angel who has to be forgiven, and then she'll ask Erna not to say anything to anybody. And Erna can't stand that kind of thing.

On the dot of six o'clock, Erika comes in, whom Erna has seen no more than two or three times so far, and calls out: 'That's it for today!'

The girls collect their things, wash their faces, apply some rouge, a bit of powder, tidy their hair, manicure their fingernails and prepare for the evening, for freedom.

Erna watches nervously, her heart is pounding. She feels so superfluous. Then Lotte pops up.

'Where are you going this evening?'

Where are you going! Yes, it's all very different from back home, where there was a schedule day and night: meals were eaten at regular times, after work she went home, her parents were waiting, there was this and that household task to be done, and even Sunday wasn't much different. The same things always happened: a walk to the nearest little town, a kind of promenade through the main streets, gossip at a girlfriend's place, work at home. Now it's all very different, she's by herself, there's nothing already arranged, she's got to organize her own time, she's got to think about where she wants to go, because she can't sit in her room all the time. What does she want to do?

'I don't really know.'

'You could come with me, but my boyfriend's waiting for me downstairs. We're going to the stadium for some sports. Are you involved in sports too?'

'I'd like to be.'

'Fine, you can come to our club. I'll take you with me on Monday.'

They walk down the stairs and across the courtyard, through the building at the front and into the street. A beautiful car is just driving away from the entrance, an open blue four-seater. Erna sees a dark scarf fluttering and light-coloured hair, and a stiff bowler hat next to it.

'Wasn't that Trude Leussner?'

'Yes. And the guy next to her was Lortzing', Lotte remarks neutrally.

'Who … ?'

'Lortzing! You know who he is!'

Lortzing … ?'

'Why are you staring like an idiot? Trude is his girlfriend. I know he can be horrible sometimes, but in my opinion he looks considerably more imposing than Siodmak. If I had to choose between Trude and Erika, I'd forget about Herr Siodmak's personal secretary. Though four hundred marks is a nice big salary.'

'How do you girls know all this stuff? I'm sure they don't tell you about it.'

'How does a dog know that he's got fleas?' Lotte is laughing.

'And they're not right for each other at all. I mean, Siodmak and Lortzing are much too old.'

'Erna, dear, you're a nice girl, but please just think sometime about how you're going to live in Berlin on your hundred and twenty marks, or whatever they're paying you.'

Lotte pulls a face. She really didn't want to say something as confrontational as that. She's very smart, but the truths she has to tell sometimes pop out a bit too quickly, and now she's sorry for Erna.

'Don't take it to heart so much.' She smiles, waving her little square hand around in front of Erna's face. 'You'll get over it. We'll talk about it later, I really don't have time now. Look over there, yes, there, I mean at the young man. Do you like him?'

She points across the street, where a young gentleman in a sporty blue suit is walking up and down. He's smoking one cigarette after another, without looking in the direction of the two girls. His hat sits at a slight angle, giving him a dashing appearance. Erna can't see his face clearly.

'That's my boyfriend.'

'Nice-looking guy.'

'Yes, isn't he? That's what I think. Well, if you come along on Monday night, I'll introduce you to him.'

Erna is glad that she can leave now, without making the young man's acquaintance. She takes a swift farewell.

Seen from behind as she strolls slowly on her well-shaped legs across the street, Lotte looks very attractive. She's always jumping from one thing to another. Of course, right away she tells her boyfriend about the 'new girl' she has befriended. Her boyfriend listens very closely. He's a bank clerk, today he had to check through an absolutely enormous account to find arithmetical errors, the numbers are still flickering before his eyes, Lotte's chatter is wonderfully soothing.

And Erna marches through the streets as they fill rapidly with office clerks, shop assistants, workers whose day is over. Doors open, shutters and windows are closed, lights go on as work continues into the evening in some offices, the factories' iron gates roll back on their tracks to clear the way, all the railway carriages are crammed full with people, sirens wail, the river of people pours into the wide roads which lead to the working-class districts and the workers' apartments. Fresh groups emerge from the side streets everywhere. They flow noisily, yet calmly, evenly through the streets. Erna is right in the middle. Her heart is pounding. She knows the way more or less now. She observes it all attentively, there are all kinds of things she hasn't seen before. Young girls are hurrying along, girls with artfully painted faces under chic hats set at daring angles. They have appointments with the young men of this city, they disappear into cafés with dance music sounding from inside, they're travelling on buses, their short, tasteful spring dresses are bright spots of colour amid the confusion. Erna has never worried particularly about her clothes, she's not vain and not the least bit demanding, but today her little world is suddenly starting to change. She'd like something different to wear.

Erna stops to look in the lovely windows of jewellers, of fashion houses. She sees prices there which amount to several months of her salary. Of course, you can make something yourself, she reflects, she had to make her own clothes quite a lot at home.

But the river carries her with it again. The traffic is getting denser. One private car after another pushes past, the high yellow buses seem to move on stilts, their crowded upper decks swaying dangerously on the fast-flowing current. The masses are dammed up at the intersections. The police officer raises a hand, everybody crosses the street. The office clerks are carrying satchels which held their breakfasts, the workers are carrying lunch pails. The girls have more spring in their steps than in the morning, their time to relax is coming, their free time, the evening. Everybody is moving quickly, because powerful gusts of wind are hissing in the dark clouds which are scudding across the city, there's rain coming, a storm, night will bring release as it washes away the warmth of the day. Nature's hasty, oppressive air forces the people to breathe differently, more heavily and uneasily, it's a curious feeling for Erna. Windows snap shut suddenly, streetlamps blaze into light, the façades of the buildings shine in the pale light of the stormy sky, blue, yellow, ghostly, threatening and unreal. You feel a longing for cozy rooms and good friends, so you can let the storm rain itself out against closed shutters.

But Erna is alone. She has nothing but her heart and her youth. She's moving in the great river, but the people are still strangers to her. The girls have cool expressions, and the men don't look at her. She's small and unremarkable, but she has pride in her heart. She's alone in this city of Berlin, an office girl, a badly paid typist, not quite nineteen years old, a girl who grew up in a strict, organized working-class world where personal ambition was never encouraged, where everything had to be subordinated to the iron laws and the unyielding will of her class. But she won't let this new, confusing world get her down.

Will she prove herself?

She's moving away from the centre, the river divides again, individuals turn off into side streets, the cinemas are filling up, the restaurants.

Trams and buses are overcrowded, the elevated trains are rumbling down the streets, lightning flashes in the black sky above it all. The thunder follows at long intervals, coming slowly, hesitantly, the storm isn't here yet.

Lights are going on in the apartment buildings, the workers are coming home, they eat, they rest.

Will I get home before it starts to rain? Erna wonders. Suddenly she wishes that she had somebody in this city whom she can trust, who belongs to her, who'll protect her. The faces of all the strangers make her nervous, the unpleasant feeling lasts for seconds at a time before it slowly passes. An attack of homesickness, a longing for her family, a moment of fear, sadness and tiredness. She walks more quickly, overtaking other pedestrians, some object to that, strangers brush past her, which street should she turn into now? The buildings are closer together and dirtier now, the brightly lit shops are disappearing, their places taken by little greengrocers' shops, bakeries, butchers' shops and bars. The river is slipping away from her, there's the side street which leads to her apartment. She'll be home in time, before the storm breaks.

That's her second day in this city, her first at the office. So today she met the girls of Berlin, some of them. Am I different? she wonders. They all want to carve out a place for themselves, by any means and at any cost, fighting in a way which she doesn't understand yet, unreservedly and uncompromisingly. So this Lotte Weissbach, barely a year older than Erna, asks her a practical question: How do you think you can live in Berlin on a hundred and twenty marks? Erna thinks about that, she does some sums, but she can't get the question out of her mind, it's unpleasant, and the answer is much too easy.

By the time she reaches the door of her building everything has turned black, and the first raindrops are falling.

A few women have gathered inside, they're standing in a circle and gossiping, pausing to listen to the noise which is coming from overhead before sticking their heads together and whispering again.

Erna has to walk through the middle, they look at her carefully, hostilely, silently, nobody replies to her 'Good evening', she climbs the stairs slowly, the women's eyes follow her.

She hears the argument too, it seems to be on her floor. The noise is getting louder and louder. A girl half-screams.

The little gas lamps give off a dull light. Lots of doors are standing open, women and children are trying to hear what's being said upstairs. The building is completely quiet for a moment. The sound from a terrible clap of thunder falls like rain. The gas lamps flicker. The landing windows are a bilious green colour.

Erna walks up quickly, taking two steps at a time, she wants to get into her room. But when she reaches the third floor the noise overhead starts up again, the sound of a blow can be heard throughout the building, a girl wails loudly, and from behind a door on the third floor a grating female voice complains: 'What a brutal man!'

'What's going on?' Erna asks.

'They're brawling again!'

Yes, Erna can hear that. She walks up the remaining flights of stairs.

'Get lost, I'll chuck you down the stairs, you bastard. Sleeping with my wife, that was a good idea, wasn't it? We won't be living under communism for a long time yet, you little snotnose!'

'If you hit the girl again, you'll regret it!'

Erna walks around the last corner, the fourth floor is in front of her. All the doors on the left-hand side are open, she can't see down the corridor, Frau Matschek's door is closed. There's a girl with messed-up hair lying on the floor, hunched right down and sobbing, outside the door in the middle, which seems to be next to Erna's apartment. A slight young man in a grey windbreaker is standing next to the wall, closest to Erna. He's holding his right arm defensively in front of his face as he looks at his opponent, who's yelling at him.

'Ha! Since when does pretty-boy tell me what to do?'

The man is tall, squarely built, but his face is pale and unhealthy, he's standing directly under a lamp, and its light is falling right onto his face. He's remarkably well-dressed for a working-class apartment building like this one, a freshly pressed black suit, a stiff hat, the ends of his moustache are turned up dashingly.

Erna cries out suddenly in fear because the man moves forward to attack and thrashes the boy, who is much weaker than he is, with his open hand. The girl cries out at the same time and kicks around with her legs, but she doesn't get up, even though she's lying right next to the attacker.

The man squeezes the boy, who's flailing around wildly, between his legs, and starts working on his head, mocking him as he does so.

'Go on, save your little doll, why don't you? What has other people's business got to do with you, hey? You'll keep your nose out of it next time!'

Erna watches, trembling, she wants this wild, unfair thrashing to stop, she presses her balled hands against her mouth in agitation. She's choking with rage and indignation, why isn't anybody helping?

A man's voice yells from above: 'Quiet!'

Then she gathers her courage, moves a step closer, she has to get into her apartment after all, grabs the unfamiliar man's arm and says: 'Please, just leave the boy alone!'

The man with the dashing moustache turns around in amazement, he probably hadn't even noticed Erna before.

'Oh! What's this scarecrow screeching about?'

Erna stands there with her head down, her eyes have become smaller, her cheeks are red with embarrassment. She looks at the young man. There's some blood trickling across his chalk-white face. She turns around and says loudly: 'Leave him alone!' The attacker, to whom the girl probably belongs, makes a mocking, contemptuous face. He's evidently considering what he should say to Erna, whether it's even worth answering her. But before he can decide, Erna hears somebody walking slowly down the stairs from the fifth floor. It's a young guy, dressed only in trousers and an open shirt. He stops, looks at everybody for a moment and suddenly starts yelling.

'Stop all that noise, the lot of you, or you'll have us to deal with!'

More residents of the building seem to have gathered upstairs.

The young guy leans over the banister, as if he wants to make sure that his orders are being carried out.

First the young girl stands up, she doesn't look up, just straightens her dress and disappears through the open door next to the Matscheks'.

Ah, so they're my neighbours, Erna thinks, the ones I already heard through those thin walls.

The young guy and his people upstairs must really be making a powerful impression on Erna's neighbour. Perhaps he decides that, with so many people against him, there's not much more he can do. He lets go of the slight young man and mutters something across the banister: 'Keep your nose out of my affairs. They're none of your damned business, got it?'

The young worker up above says nothing. He just looks at the man and smiles contemptuously.

The well-dressed brawler turns around, spits on the floor, and waves his hand through the air. There's foam on his lips, he looks epileptic. Without saying anything else, he goes into his apartment, where the girl went, and closes the door behind him.

Erna sighs with relief. She looks towards the boy, who's wiping his face with a handkerchief, managing only to spread the blood more widely.

'Are you hurt?'

'No, it's nothing to worry about.'

He walks slowly down the corridor, there's a door open at the end, but before he disappears into the apartment the young guy up above says, in a loud but not unfriendly voice: 'You've got to think of something else, Köhler. If you get into a fight with that bastard you'll get smashed every time.'

Erna is nodding vigorously, that's exactly what she thinks.

The boy doesn't say anything, just shrugs his shoulders and goes into his apartment. Erna runs quickly down the corridor, unlocks her door and crashes into Frau Matschek, who's been eavesdropping for sure.

'Well, whaddaya say to that?'

Then she walks straight into Erna's room and starts giving chapter and verse.

Erna's tired. She sits down on the bed and props her hands under her chin.

'The man next door, he's called Berger. The point is, he's not even married to the girl. Living in sin, as they say. He's a classy one, I'm telling you! Nothing to do with me, and I don't pay any attention either. Not in the least! The man earns a lot, but he's a bad apple. Nobody really knows where he works. Well, I don't pay any attention to other people! Hands off is what I always say! If you look at it in a proper light, it's the girl's own fault, isn't it? I mean, why did she get involved with Köhler, of all people? 'Cos he's in the Red Front, an actual Communist. I mean the one who just got slapped around. He used to work for AEG in Oberschöneweide, then they chucked him out. Now he's unemployed. Well, he deserves it, that one does …'

Erna looks up disapprovingly, old mother Matschek's whispering dies away.

'Frau Matschek, please leave me alone now, I'm very tired.'

Erna gets up, she can't stand the old girl anymore.

'Well, I only wanted to set you straight. 'Cos if you mess with Berger you'll get into trouble soon enough, mark my words. But anyway, no offence.'

The old girl slams the door.

Window open!

Outside the rain is falling in the darkness of the town, releasing the tension. The storm is coming down in long gusts. The rain is hissing a comforting tune. Erna won't turn on the light yet. The air at the window is cooler and fresher. Lights are shimmering in the buildings. That's night in the city.

She combs her hair and stares into the darkness, eyes wide open. She passes her hands closely before her eyes, strong, vigorous, nice-smelling hands.

She hears voices next door, individual words are clearly distinguishable. The building is settling down, the eavesdropping doors are being closed, the people are sitting down to eat. The gramophone starts playing again. The rain hisses. The little girl sits on the windowsill and stares out into the unfamiliar city. She breathes its air, she has to; its life grabs her and draws her in; its people already hate her and love her. She reacts simply and decisively to everything. She knows that the rain will fade away again, that the night will come and then the morning. She knows that she'll have to work again and to learn, because she's alone and doesn't want to go under, a little unknown girl, a girl from the provinces.

No.

She turns on the light, takes her Sunday dress out of her suitcase and starts sewing. She alters and repairs. She's got to have a pretty, up-to-date dress which she can wear at the office and on the street. Of course, then she won't have a dress for Sundays anymore, but she doesn't care about that at the moment.

While she's fishing around in the suitcase, she comes upon an old-fashioned soft bonnet which she'd put between layers of clothes to stop them wrinkling. What can she do with it? When she starts working on it, she doesn't quite know how she wants it to turn out. She cuts off the strings and sews some seams together and tries it on in the mirror and gets a shock. There's a confident face looking out at her under the kind of fabulous hat you see pictures of in the up-to-date fashion magazines. The felt clings around her head and slants over her nose. There's only one eye, it's shimmering and has a veil around it, a breath of intriguing air. She has given herself a shock.

She works late into the night. Outside the rain is still streaming down, the room is cooler. Sometimes you can hear a car horn in the distance, a soft, muted, comforting sound. Then she has a wash, freshens up by splashing her whole body with cold water, does a few exercises, and collapses into bed.

She sleeps deeply and dreamlessly, but after five hours she has to get up again.

Somebody's ringing the doorbell for the apartment, Frau Matschek shuffles along the hallway, the milkman rattles the cans, the door is closed again.

Erna stretches in bed. The things she was working on overnight are still lying there, the hat and the dress. The sun is shining on them, everything looks nice and attractive. What would Mother have to say if she knew that her daughter was wearing her good, her only Sunday dress on working days!

Erna buffs her low-heeled shoes to a brilliant shine, puts on the dress and some new stockings, and the hat on top. But when Frau Matschek knocks with the morning coffee, Erna tears off her hat again and hides it. She doesn't try it on again until the old girl has disappeared.

Another little piece will have to be cut off on the side, to show her hair to full advantage. Poised on her toes, her hands on her narrow waist, her head a little to the side, Erna examines herself critically in the mirror. And then she has an inspiration. She takes off the hat again, combs the hair at the front straight down and, her mind soon made up, takes her scissors and cuts herself a fringe. Her flaming red hair now flows out from the hat over her forehead, you can't see her freckles anymore, the ugly Erna has disappeared. Hooray!

Today is Thursday, her third day in Berlin. The sun is shining outside, and Erna completely forgets to check her watch. She drinks her coffee hastily standing up, one hand holding the cup, the other collecting her sewing kit and throwing it into the suitcase, then she tidies her room a bit and rushes out.

Maybe she would still have got to the office on time if there hadn't been another incident in the stairwell.

Erna spots him from one floor up. She recognizes him immediately, the boy from last night who was beaten up by her neighbour, the one Frau Matschek didn't like because he was a Communist. He's wearing the same windbreaker and apparently doesn't recognize her, although he glances at her face. Erna says 'Good morning' quietly as she walks past him.

She's got as far as the street door when he stops and calls out 'Hey!' She turns around. But she has to be at the office in ten minutes.

'I didn't recognize you at all! You're lodging at Frau Matschek's, aren't you?' Some kind of lung disease, Erna decides. She's familiar with such faces.

'That was nice of you, last night.'

'Ach, I couldn't help you, unfortunately.'

'No, not much chance of that. But still, don't take this the wrong way, if you ever need somebody you can come to me. I mean, if you ever need advice or help, 'cos I don't have anything else to offer you … No, no, don't say that! People get into trouble all the time. I suppose you're thinking that I'm too young? I'm all of thirty, Fräulein, and I've already been around a bit and dealt with all kinds of things. But I don't want to hold you up, I suppose you have to get to work?'

The odd conversations and acquaintanceships are mounting up, Erna tells herself. Now she's got somebody who wants to give her advice for free, she has to laugh. But the young man says that he's thirty years old? She'd never have thought it.

All kinds of things happen in these buildings, we live without knowing anything about the people in the apartment next door, their cry for help dies away, maybe we can learn something from them, and we don't ask. We're ashamed. We ignore our neighbour.

A clock strikes.

Eight times.

Naturally, the young man has ruined her last chance of getting to the office on time. She's sweating, and her heart is pounding. A nice mess that'll be.

Nobody sees her in Iron Processing Co.'s building. She makes it to the typists' room unmolested.

Thank God, she thinks, as she pulls open the door. The girls separate quickly, everybody hurries to her seat. They'd all been gathered around Trude Leussner.

'God, you gave us such a fright!'

'Hey, you should tell us when you're coming!'

Erna is still standing in the doorway. She's beaming as she walks into the room.

'Take a look at Erna! She's really dolled herself up!'

Elsbeth Siewertz is the first to notice Erna's transformation. Yes, now the other girls turn around too. That can't be yesterday's Erna, the stylish dress and the wonderful hat …

'Did anybody notice that I was late?'

'No, just get your hat and coat off, or the boss will come in and catch you.'

Lotte Weissbach and Erika Tümmler are absent again, they're working in their own rooms.

The girls look at Erna very closely. New, stylish clothes always get their attention.

'I made the dress and the hat myself.'

'Whaaat … ?'

Erna pretends it's no big deal, but she's very proud, at least now somebody realizes what she can do. The girls change their opinion of this unprepossessing little girl from the provinces quickly and completely, although they don't think much about their change of attitude. What registers with them is that something new has happened. They look with their eyes and listen with their ears and smell with their noses, anything beyond that is somebody else's problem.

Lotte sticks her head through the door.

'Did Erna get here yet? … Erna! Look at you! Come here … !'

She's delighted, clapping her hands, Erna has to get up. Lotte feels the material, sums it up, criticizes, and then when somebody fetches the hat from the cloakroom, Lotte's eyes and her whole face light up with genuine enthusiasm.

'Wow, you must make me a hat like that too!'

The typewriters are going tap-tap-tap, the words are flying through the room, one of the girls is keeping a watch outside to prevent any surprise visits by Lortzing or Siodmak.

A few girls are sitting at Trude Leussner's desk again and whispering to her. Something must be up there! Just what has got into them? Trude, the quiet, reserved Trude, is telling them something ...

'Look at the bottom here, I'd rearrange the material, that would definitely be cuter ...'

Lotte could discuss the dress for hours yet, but she has to get back to her office in a hurry to look after the telephone. She drags Erna into the corridor with her and puts on a portentous face. Yes, something really is up.

'Trude has had a bust-up with Lortzing!'

She's beaming as she says it.

'What do you think of that?'

Erna doesn't know what she should think of that.

'When you've done your work, come over to my office.'

Lotte dashes to her office, and Erna goes back to her typewriter. Her head is starting to swim.

'Listen, girls', Eva says, 'yesterday Siodmak dictated this letter to head office to me, and all I can say is that he was sweating blood the whole time. Because they were complaining that his calculations don't add up. They add up alright, he says. Look at this', holding up her steno pad and showing it around, 'that'll be five typed pages. I always get the long letters, because of course the other young ladies always run for cover ...'

'Well, a girl with a face like yours won't get worked to death', Elsbeth says.

Erna bashes away on her Orga Privat. It's quite an old model, and can be heard above all the other typewriters in the room.

Trude Leussner is sitting in front of Erna. She's talking with animation and force, which she never does otherwise. She has drawn up her legs, the light-coloured skirt is tight across her knees, which look rosy, strong and healthy through her sheer stockings. Erna hears a few things here and there. Trude is laughing at Lortzing. The girls are listening attentively.

Then Erna sees something unexpected which gives her a bit of a shock, she can't explain it. It's Lieselotte Kries, who's sitting right next to Trude, and has even put her left arm around Trude's shoulder and is looking openly and unconcernedly into her unheeding face.

'He danced with other girls the whole night. I hadn't been looking for ages, and suddenly he's standing at my table again and wanting to introduce me to another gentleman, a business acquaintance. Are you talking to me, I said …'

Then Lotte Weissbach tells another version of the story.

'She wanted a fur coat, but he didn't buy it for her … No, it's not what you think. Trude isn't the least bit bothered if Lortzing goes out with other girls. Look', snapping her fingers, 'a different one every night for all she cares! Only he has to pay. But you know, Erna', whispering softly, 'I think there's something else behind it. Trude never used to get sick. And I've known her for as long as she's worked here. No, you can't fool me.'

'Can't we help her?'

Lotte dangles her thick legs.

'I suppose you always want to play the angel who saves us all? Every girl has to work things out for herself. Or don't you think so?'

No, Erna doesn't agree, but she doesn't say anything. Still, for lots of reasons Lotte passes on what Erna says to her, and one or another of the girls looks at the little typist at the Orga Privat in a new way.

At lunchtime they go to the dining hall again, Lotte, Erna, Martha, and Trude too. When Lieselotte hears that Trude Leussner is going along, she joins them as well. Erna has the distinct, and for her uncomfortable, feeling that Lieselotte is afraid.

As if she would tell secrets!

When they eat, the girls are quite cheerful at first. Trude talks about Lortzing again, amusingly and as if it's nothing. Erna doesn't quite know if she's playacting or not. Trude's eyes are glittering feverishly, she's talking rapidly and excitedly. Erna feels instinctively that something's not right there.

Of course, the food doesn't taste particularly good today, haven't the others noticed? She's already got a stomach ache, Trude says.

Erna changes places with Martha so that she's sitting next to Trude. She leans over to her. 'Just don't think about the guy anymore.' She's sorry for the girl. Trude has such sad, clouded eyes. Maybe she really loves Herr Lortzing, and now it's all over. They'll have to console her.

'I just want to finish telling you the story, how it turned out. I mean, at the beginning he was really nice. And he always told me everything, so I knew what was happening in the company kind of at first hand. But now he's always telling dirty jokes, well, you all know what I mean …'

Trude rubs her stomach. She wants to let it all out, she says. But her face is pale, as if she's sick. She tries to smile.

'… yeah, then last night, I had no intention of sitting there the whole evening like an old maid, if you know what I mean, so towards eleven o'clock I just packed it up. Usually that's the time when it's just starting to get nice. I hadn't said anything to him at all, that made him really furious. Just picked up my things from the cloakroom and pushed off. Right, then he catches up to me at the door and wants to escort me home, all correct and polite. Then he got scared and tried to lay on the charm. Don't incur any unnecessary expenditures, I told him …'

Trude, who has never told the other girls anything about her private affairs before, is explaining herself thoroughly today, accurate down to the last detail.

As if by prior agreement, the girls listen in silence.

'… this morning he didn't pick me up in his jalopy either, not that I expected him to. Maybe he'll go out driving with his wife again …'

'What, he's married?' Erna bursts out.

The girls nod.

'Of course, so's Siodmak, that doesn't mean anything in particular.'

Trude coughs hard and spits into her handkerchief.

'Listen, if I were you, I'd go to the doctor.'

'Ach, not much point. I'm quite healthy, it'll pass.'

The conversation seems to have petered out. They feel the tiredness which follows the meal. Rest, doze, sleep.

Erna can't understand the girls. She turns over in her mind whether she should tell them so. She already knows what she wants to say.

'You know', she says quietly to them, 'I've only been here a few days and I don't know you all properly either, but the way I see it, these admirers of yours wouldn't make me happy. Why don't you try to find some boys who are your type ...'

'Ach, do you think we don't consult our own tastes? No need to worry. That's got nothing to do with what we've been talking about, they're two different things ...'

'How do you mean?'

Now Lotte jumps in.

'Look, you're getting Erna all confused. Listen, Erna, I've already explained. With the little bit of money you earn at work, you can't afford anything, or not much! But you don't need to worry that the way these girls tell it – Ready, Set, Go! – means that they've got a screw loose. I do quite well, and I like my boyfriend, and he likes me, so what's the big problem? Of course he's got to pay when we go out somewhere, but really, that goes without saying ...'

'That's not what I meant.'

'You meant me, didn't you?' Trude asks.

'Stop this, now!' Martha Hummel is drumming her fingers on the table. She's furious, but she has a completely calm, quiet voice, firm and vigorous.

'Now you're all going to start talking again about how you'd starve to death if you didn't have your admirers! I know as well as you do that our salaries are garbage and we'll never get anywhere in that joint. But all this showing off is just as bad, with some of you it's becoming intolerable. That's right, let somebody say it to your faces! Theatres, car rides, wine and all the other silly nonsense, you're always singing the same song. You've got long stories to tell every day, and Monday morning is the absolute worst. The only good thing is that most of it is hot air. Did you hear little Annemie shooting her mouth off yesterday about eating caviar? Well, it made my day to hear Otti cut her down to size. Because you're all making a tiny mistake! Erna has worked it out alright. And if a girl isn't very shrewd or very superficial, she'll get caught in a great big mess. I mean, we've already seen that happen a few times.'

'So which of us is living this way you're raving about?'

'Lotte, you know as well as I do what kinds of stories you girls always tell, and even if you're only making yourselves important, that's just as stupid. But really, we don't want to kid ourselves …'

'Well, we might … !'

They all turn around. The red-headed girl has cut into the conversation from the next table, she's been listening, she says hello to everybody because she knows the girls from Iron Processing Co.

'Why are you so afraid all of a sudden? When Martha starts sounding off, everybody's too scared to say Boo. So answer her! None of you agrees with her little sermon! Why don't you tell her? Because Martha is completely wrong!'

'Yeah, I know what you're going to say', Martha says to the red-headed Hilde with a friendly laugh, 'but what they're doing isn't nice.'

Hilde opens her eyes wide and rattles a spoon on the table, her voice sounds almost like a man's.

'Firstly self-respect, secondly instinct, thirdly shrewdness, fourthly pride. Then there are some girls who do anything for a movie ticket …'

A plump, friendly girl at the next table interjects something, apparently she has summed up the services rendered in exchange for a movie ticket in a few specific, unambiguous expressions. Erna didn't understand, but the girls laugh.

'Nah, none of it's easy', Lotte says.

'But we're still young. We'd be pretty stupid if we didn't take advantage of that. We'll regret it when it's too late. There was a little girl in our office last year, maybe you knew her, she always acted so proper, with clean underclothes and little white collars like an innocent angel …'

Hilde starts telling a story, a long story about a girl who got what she wanted shrewdly and ruthlessly and is married to a stinking rich man now. The others listen attentively, only Martha objects. She doesn't like such touching stories, she says. But Hilde won't be diverted. Erna looks at the beautiful girl in quiet admiration. Her clearly defined mouth curves forward, long lashes cover her lovely eyes, her skin is powdered a smooth white and her eyes are slightly shadowed.

This face pleases Erna, it's so frank, open and courageous, you can look at it for a long time. But this gentle red mouth is talking about things which Erna never heard before. Back home, things sometimes turned bad between boys and girls, but if a girl was expecting a baby then there had to be a marriage, otherwise the boy would have had something to deal with. But Hilde is talking about the most awful things with the aim of showing the other girls how to behave in the terrible situations they'll get into whether they want to or not.

They've moved the two tables close together, everybody is sitting tensely and listening attentively.

The radio announcer's voice trickles monotonously from the loudspeaker.

Erna looks around, searching for Trude. The girl is sitting a little apart, and hasn't participated in the conversation for quite a while. What's wrong with her? Trude is leaning forward in her chair and pressing her handkerchief to her mouth. Erna gets up quickly to help her.

'Come on, should I get you some water?'

The other girls look up.

Trude says nothing at all. She just points to the door.

Erna guides her to the washroom. When they get there, Trude vomits. Erna holds her tight and tries to calm her. All her lunch has come back up.

Erna fetches some water quickly and gets the kitchen to give her a cloth. Carefully, she wipes Trude's face clean.

'Come on, rinse out your mouth … Good.'

Trude leans on the wall, exhausted, she's breathing rapidly, her face is white and drawn, suddenly she looks ugly; ugly, fearful, harassed. She holds fast to Erna's shoulders and starts to cry. She sobs like a little child. Erna strokes her thick hair slowly.

'You've got to tell me what's wrong! You've got to get well again.'

'I've already tried everything.'

'What do you mean?'

Trude just cries and swallows.

'It's nice of you', she says, 'to take care of me like this, but I can't tell you anything now.'

'You'll have to tell me everything sometime, I'm sure I can help you.'

'Oh, it's all so horrible. And I'm only twenty years old. Why did all this have to happen to me?'

Erna frowns, her face is very serious, she knows the score now.

'Come on, let's go back in. And you'll come to my place tomorrow. Right? Promise me. And listen now: Don't do any more silly things!'

Trude looks up quickly.

'What do you mean?'

Her eyes widen as they fill with tears; she's afraid and distrustful, and wants to take back what she just said.

'You know exactly what I mean. You'll ruin yourself that way, Trude. Don't do anything stupid, we'll help you alright.'

They go back in; the girls act as if nothing in particular has happened. There you are, eating so quickly! Lots of people can't digest dining-hall food.

The lunchbreak is over. They say their goodbyes and head off in different directions, to Alexander Square, to Landsberg Street, to Frankfurt Street.

The girls from Iron Processing Co. link arms, Lotte's telling jokes, they cheer up again, and Lieselotte even suggests an excursion on the river to Werder on Sunday.

An excursion to Werder? That would be just lovely! Of course, all the girls from the office will want to join in. They'll set off in the morning and spend the whole day there. Though it's not the right season, when the trees have their spring colours, quite yet, but if the sun's shining like it is today, it'll be lovely.

As soon as they get back to the office, they tell the other girls about Lieselotte's suggestion. Everybody is all fired up. They'll buy food together, so bread and butter and cheese and sausage and all the other things they'll need, and then they'll want to get on the boat early in the morning, maybe in Caputh or Potsdam.

Every girl has a new suggestion, they're fired up and talking animatedly. Nobody pays any attention to Trude, who's sitting apart again, proud and unapproachable, not joining in the conversation. She doesn't look at Erna even once.

Of course, Elsbeth Siewertz puts herself forward again.

'Erna will have to take her Orga Privat, we'll use it to play tunes on the boat', she says.

The windows are open. Warm air is flowing in from outside. None of the girls is typing, they're talking to each other, and in their enthusiasm some of them are dancing around.

At which point Lortzing enters.

He looks around the room, and grimaces. The girls sit down in a hurry, the typewriters start hammering away all at once, but still there's a kind of odd silence in the room. Lortzing remains standing in the doorway, looking at these eleven girls' backs, and then says in his quiet, lazy voice: 'You're too well-off!'

That's all.

The girls can hear the birds singing in the garden outside, and the branches rustling. They want to go to Werder on Sunday.

'... Anybody who doesn't like it here only has to say so. Go ahead! There's the door.'

Erna looks at him.

'You of all people can afford to slack off, of course!'

With a sudden movement, he closes the door.

Erna types away grimly. Alright, she thinks, if you don't like me, the feeling is mutual. Do you know what I'll say if you come in again? And she comes up with all kinds of things. But then her thoughts take a different turn. Being singled out like that has depressed her a little, even if she doesn't want to admit it to herself. After all, she might have to pay a price for Lortzing's dislike. Being unemployed in Berlin isn't an inviting prospect for a little girl like her.

Oh well, she thinks at last, resignedly.

Evening comes, the girls leave the building.

Lieselotte puts her arm through Erna's right away.

'We live in Schöneberg, Innsbruck Street. Right next to the park. We can take the train almost to the door.'

The evening is still pleasant. They walk through the crowded streets, Lieselotte finds things to point out and explain everywhere, she knows some people in the train carriage, girls and young men, she's got lots of things to gossip about and she can make them sound exciting. The journey passes very quickly.

Lieselotte's apartment really is in a nice position. The two rooms and kitchen are on the third floor of a big building with a wide front and a very elegant façade.

Lieselotte switches on the radio straight away.

'Would you like to dance?'

'I'm not very good.'

'Well, come on, we'll try.' And she promptly puts her arms gently around Erna and glides through the apartment with her. She leads decisively and vigorously, it's easy for Erna to follow, she's enjoying this. They move towards the open window in the entryway, church bells are ringing outside, you can look into the distance across the sea of buildings. The white furniture is suffused with the pink evening light, everything looks cloying and unreal.

The announcer says: 'That was a piece from Straus's *Waltz Dream* ...'

'Pretty, wasn't it?'

They laugh. Erna's happy. She wishes she had an apartment like this too, and a nice husband. Then she'd enjoy going to work and earning money for the household. So Lieselotte really ought to be very happy. Funny girl ... She can see a long way across the square, across the big city. Lieselotte explains to her where the Cathedral is and the Parliament and Prenzlau Avenue. Erna hops up happily, whistling.

'Have a seat. Right, take a look at our family album. I'll be right back ...'

Lieselotte flits about, starts brewing coffee which Erna is looking forward to, apologizes for this or that, and calls out things from the kitchen to Erna, who is sitting in the 'parlour', talking to her about everything except her dubious relationship with Lortzing. Erna, who in her childlike naïveté had expected a full confession, is pleased. She would have been embarrassed if Lieselotte had started in on that, and she listens patiently to the harmless chatter. At the moment, Lieselotte is talking about her 'Manni'.

'My Manni isn't here tonight. The bank clerks have a kind of little club which meets once a week. On Sundays they go on excursions, I've gone a few times too, it's always tremendously nice. But the men much prefer to keep to themselves. They can have it too! For all I care! We don't need them, do we, Erna?'

She pours the coffee and looks at Erna so sincerely with her gentle, moist doe eyes that the little girl has to nod.

'He's coming home very late again tonight. If you'd been here yesterday you'd have met him, but on his beer-drinking evenings I always assume that I'll already be in bed before he gets back …'

Lieselotte pulls on a close-fitting wool sweater which shows her curves even more clearly.

'You know, Erna, I'd really like to get a position as a secretary in the bank where my Manni works, then I'd really be able to put some money by. At the moment I've got to count every penny. That's why we haven't had a child yet. You hope every day that something will turn up, don't you? Do you get that kind of bee in your bonnet sometimes too? Maybe you'd like to get into the movies?'

Erna thinks about it.

'No, that's never occurred to me.'

'Or if a girl had a rich boyfriend!'

'But you've got your husband.'

'Ach, you know, maybe that wouldn't even bother him. You don't understand, do you? You know, I envy you a little, but put yourself in my shoes for a minute. Look, I've been married for two years now, a lot can change in two years. My father had died, and I was all alone. My husband's a good man, and at least I had something to be going on with. Of course, he knows quite well that I don't want to stay in this poky little apartment forever. And that's why he buys lottery tickets. Of course, it's all a matter of chance. We bought that toaster there the time we won fifty marks. It's a pity that we only bought a one-eighth share.'

They walk through the rooms and look at everything, the sheets and towels, the furniture, the crockery, and finally the clothes. Lieselotte takes out a long white voile dress with colourful trim.

'You make such nice things for yourself. Look at this rag, I don't know what to do with it anymore. You can have it if you like … No, take it, it doesn't fit me anymore anyway.'

No, Erna doesn't want to accept it, she really doesn't, the idea makes her uncomfortable. But Lieselotte is acting as if it will be a relief to her to clear her wardrobe out a bit.

At that moment, somebody rings the doorbell.

The two girls look at each other.

'Surely that's not my husband? No, he has his key. It'll only be a beggar.'

They continue their inspection of the fabric. Erna is surprised that Lieselotte doesn't go to see who's at the door.

Suddenly the doorbell rings again, quietly and almost hesitantly.

'Let me, I'll look', Erna says. Lieselotte has suddenly turned white, her mouth is hanging open.

Erna goes to the door.

An elegant young man looks at her, considerably taken aback.

'Is Frau Kries at home?' he asks rather uncertainly. He's wearing a light blue summer suit and a soft hat. The tie matches the colour of the suit perfectly.

Lieselotte hurries to the door, she speaks rapidly, but without looking at the young man.

'Ah, Alfred! May I present: Fräulein Halbe from our office – Herr Sommerfeld, a friend of my husband's.'

They drink coffee together. The young man is very quiet at first, glancing at Lieselotte again and again, but Lieselotte has a lot to do in the kitchen, so he has to converse with Erna. He's a nice guy, polite, polished and obliging, he can chat pleasantly. Erna feels that she should contribute, and asks why he isn't out with the other bank clerks. He's puzzled for a moment, but fortunately Lieselotte comes in with fresh coffee.

Time passes, the young gentleman has been sitting next to Erna for half an hour already. Lieselotte is in the kitchen almost the whole time, she has to make supper. He's got to go now. Erna definitely doesn't want to stay any longer either.

Suddenly somebody turns the key in the door outside. Herr Sommerfeld gives Erna an uneasy and embarrassed look, as if she could tell him who's coming now.

Then Lieselotte rushes in, lowers her nervous, confused, resentful face to the pair and whispers: 'My Manni! You're Erna's husband! Herr Halbe! Got it?!'

She rushes out again, and they hear her high, calm voice outside.

'Manni, we have visitors, quite a surprise ... yes ... but why are you home this early? ... I see ...'

Erna is staring, she still hasn't quite caught on.

The young gentleman is contemplating the pictures on the wall, calmly and intently.

Enter Herr Kries.

Erna hadn't pictured the man to herself like that at all. Short, fat and jovial, you'd put his age at thirty-eight, never twenty-eight. He's got some funny curls on his otherwise rather bare head. He greets his guests in a very friendly and obliging manner.

Erna can't help thinking of something which happened that morning at the office. Administration received a visit from a man whose luxuriant hair prompted Lotte Weissbach to remark that the gentleman evidently liked to see curls on the pillow. Erna didn't know the expression, so she was told a nice story: At one time, Trude Leussner wanted to get her plaits cut off, but encountered opposition from Lortzing, who confided to her that her hair looked charming on the white pillow. Of course, Trude repeated this in the office, and now 'He likes to see curls on the pillow' was a popular and oft-used expression among the girls. So Erna can't help remembering it when she sees Herr Kries.

Lieselotte introduces her visitors, her voice is loud, her cheeks are red: 'My new friend from the office, Erna Halbe, and her husband!'

Herr Kries is pleased to meet them, he's not particularly surprised and invites them to join him and his wife for supper, but Erna has to go, she really must go.

She takes her leave and walks quickly down the stairs, across the street, accompanied by Herr Sommerfeld, whose name is actually neither Halbe nor Sommerfeld. He doesn't say anything, and she doesn't say anything either. What's she supposed to say, anyway? She walks through some streets which she's never seen before, straight ahead all the way, and she's only surprised that the young gentleman is walking quietly beside her.

Finally she decides that it's too ridiculous, she turns a little to the side and asks sharply: 'So what's your name?'

He introduces himself: 'Wolf Tümmler.'

Tümmler? Tümmler? The name sounds somewhat familiar to Erna, ah yes, Erika Tümmler, and eventually it turns out that this is her brother.

He also met Lieselotte through Erika, and of course everything was very embarrassing, but …

'I don't want to know anything about it', Erna says brusquely.

What'll she do now? She wants to go home, she wants him to point out the right tram to her, and then he can fade away.

Yes, Lieselotte, she thinks, she can't see things as she should, she lets herself drift along without reaching any particular destination, because all she wants to do is earn lots of money. I'll do it differently.

'Are you still angry with me?' Wolf Tümmler asks.

She doesn't quite know what to say.

'That's our tennis court over there, may I invite you, maybe we could chat for a while longer in the club café?'

Erna looks at him wide-eyed, what's he playing at?

'Incidentally, my sister will be there too.'

'Erika?'

'Yes. She's told me about you. You've only just come to Berlin, haven't you?'

There's open land behind the apartment buildings, trees and dense undergrowth behind wooden fences, there are some villas, they already have a summery glow, well cared for gardens, wrought-iron gates, gravel paths.

The broken-up, uncultivated building land is interspersed with wooden fences, there's a little door open here, you can see through to some sports fields. Two sets of football goalposts and nets, the posts painted a light colour, stand at opposite ends of a saturated, dirty-looking grey-green field, an old man carrying a big shovel is walking across it. Wolf Tümmler walks past the goalposts and keeps going, he points diagonally across the street. Above a high wire-mesh fence you can see a building, not much taller than the wire, which is painted bright pink. At the entrance there's a white sign showing the tennis club's name in big black letters. There are some elegant cars waiting at the side of the road. The daylight has gone now, the evening wind is blowing across the trees nearby, lights are coming on, the gentle air of the early, warm evening envelops everything, there's a touch of coolness, of melancholy. The white balls are still flying around the courts, at long intervals a player's shout splits the quiet air, a girl laughs. The shouts die away only slowly.

Erna stops and looks. The young man watches her, smiling. Maybe he's sensitive, and is hoping to make his peace with this girl whose acquaintance he made in such embarrassing circumstances. But Erna isn't worried about her companion anymore, to her he's a good-looking young man, polite, obliging, evidently Lieselotte Kries's lover, but otherwise completely uninteresting. He takes her onto the club's grounds. She walks calmly beside him, he takes off his hat several times, the people at the tables acknowledge his greetings and follow the pair with their eyes.

'It's a big set-up', he explains, 'there are some more courts behind this building, and a garage for the cars down here.'

The ground floor of the club café even has a buffet, a waiter is running up the stairs. The upper floor of the café is crowded. Young people dressed for sports, the girls in kasha satin blouses, sweaters and pleated skirts, the men in white trousers and roomy shirts, are sitting among the elegant guests who have come in more formal clothes. They're drinking tea and chocolate, conversing, flirting, and some of them are dancing. There's a gramophone in one corner, they've made a bit of room, moved the tables aside, now they're dancing in the narrow space. Erna doesn't like the people, they're all staring at her, she hears quite clearly when a young man makes a remark about her and the girls at his table giggle at it. Idiots, Erna thinks, I'm definitely not coming here again. She doesn't have any money either, and she doesn't want Wolf Tümmler to order anything for her. She goes up to the gramophone, leans against the wall and looks around. Some of the girls look fresh and young, she likes them. Dresses with red and blue stripes are glowing around the room, the colours look bold and crisp next to each other, the dresses are short, the girls have long, strong legs, it's all pretty and pleasant. Erika is part of it too. An older gentleman with silver-grey hair is sitting at her table. When the gramophone stops playing, he kisses her hand and leaves. Wolf Tümmler waves to his sister.

'Where did you two spring up from?'

'Your friend Lieselotte introduced us.'

'I see.'

Erika looks thoughtful. A young man claps Wolf Tümmler on the shoulder. 'Hello!' he says. The two move a little bit to the side.

'Do you like it here?' Erika asks.

'No, not at all.'

'Oh, whyever not?' Erika looks attentive, she pulls up a chair for Erna and orders coffee, then they sit back a bit and talk. Erika isn't dancing anymore. First she wants to find out why her brother has turned up with this little one.

Wolf Tümmler walks past at one point, but when he sees the two girls deep in conversation, he fades away again without drawing attention to himself.

It's getting late. The lamps are shining more brightly. A cool moon swims through the air. People move to different tables. Erika's clever eyes linger over the simple face of this Orga Privat Girl, who is so quiet and inconspicuous at the office, and can say such intelligent things here. Wolf Tümmler? Erna isn't interested in meeting men? Erika has to laugh, she wishes her brother was sitting next to her now. And she's curious about what the little one might have to tell her.

Later these two unusual girls are sitting by themselves in a corner of the club café in Wilmersdorf, on a white balcony under the vault of the night sky, beautiful, gentle and radiant. Stars flicker like fireflies through the trembling air. Friedenau is out there, Steglitz, Dahlem, the river Havel. You can hear light, cheerful dance music from the houses, lanterns blaze up, distant shouts fade softly into the heat of the night. Insects and moths bump into the lamps. Everything is turning summery. Iced coffee. Pleasant air. Silence. Talk ....

Erna, a short, stocky girl with rather thin legs, healthy, almost nineteen years old and starting out in life, what can she have to talk about? You'll be able to see these stars above her hometown too. There are fewer than ten thousand people in Korbetha, but the trains stop there. The carriages are shunted day and night, the long-distance express waits, but nobody gets out. The apprentice waiters in the station restaurant call to each other beneath a dark sky, thousands of rails intersect, a signal is raised, whistles, that's Korbetha. The chemical works in Leuna, which feel near enough to touch, breathe their poison into the little workers' housing estate, into a little low-roofed terraced house which gives shelter to three families with all their children. 'Do you know how they live there?' the little one asks. 'They get up at five in the morning in the dirty tenements, the lights are already burning everywhere on the estate, and the men walk out into the grey morning with their lunch pails and haversacks, through the long streets, to the mines and factories. And I went with them, yes, Erika, I used to work in a factory. And you all pull such faces when you talk about 'factory girls'! You all want to get to the top, as quickly and easily as possible, but you need to spend a couple of years in the kind of dumps I've been in before you know what the road to the top looks like. I couldn't bear it in the factory, I became a steno-typist. Quite a few people believe that's different. They always want to climb higher and higher, and suddenly there's a crash, and they're right down the bottom again. Now, I don't believe that, say, Lieselotte Kries is as terribly happy as she always makes out. Yes, of course, I came to Berlin to try my luck too. Maybe one day I'll earn lots of money, then I'll go back and help my mother, and my brothers and sisters. I belong with them, not here, that's something I'll never forget. My ambitions are much more modest than you other girls', and I know more or less how far we can get. I was attracted to Berlin. That was always my great dream, to travel, to see the world, to look around … Of course, I knew that I wouldn't get anything handed to me on a plate. But I thought I'd have more opportunities here. And I've learned a lot in these first few days too, more than a lot. There are quite a few things I don't understand. You know, you're all a long way ahead of me in some things, you know more and you have no illusions, but still, quite a few of you make me sad. Don't you think too that lots of them will be disappointed, maybe some of them very badly? Why is that? They're fumbling and searching and drifting, they don't have anything solid to hold onto, and only a few of them are completely happy …'

'Are you?'

'Yes, I'm satisfied with what I am. I'm not wishing for too much and I'll never forget that thousands of people have much worse problems than I do. And if I slip up here, I'll go back home. Of course, I'd prefer to live comfortably too, but not at any price …'

Erika, a calm, proud girl with a beautiful, supple figure, healthy, twenty-six years old and earning a salary of four hundred marks a month, started on sixty marks herself. Yes, she thinks, Erna might well be right, but anybody who lives in Berlin looks at these things differently. Anybody who has ever been hungry takes one risk after another. There's lots happening in a big city, there are beautiful things, other people live well and comfortably, the girls are sought after. So a girl meets men, loves some and tolerates the others, often the differences aren't so big after all. Anybody with a sensitive nature always runs the risk that there'll be a big blow-up sometime. 'You've got to be in damned good shape', Erika says, 'to deal with that sort of thing. Not just in yourself personally, of course, it's all nonsense. I'll tell you something that happened to me once. I was fed up with it all. During the hyperinflation. I couldn't bear the streets and the job anymore, and least of all the men, even though I had some money. I remember that we were having a very warm spell. Nothing mattered to me anymore. So I went out one evening and swam across Müggel Lake, all the way across – though I'm not a particularly good swimmer. I wouldn't really have cared if I'd gone under. When I got out, I was shot to pieces. Then I slept, slept for ages, I felt in good shape again. You see, I play tennis. I can even drive a car now. I can do anything if I have to ...'

The stars are wandering across the sky, you can feel a chilly, alert silence from around the river Havel, locomotives are whistling, in the street nearby you can hear a car horn, in the distance glasses are rattling ...

'Yes, you're right, of course, sport and books or whatever it is, it doesn't always work. That time when I'd lost all hope, when I didn't know what I was knocking myself out for' – she puts her right arm gently on Erna's shoulder – 'that's when I met Georg, one of my brother's friends, a young student who had no money at all and lived from whatever work he could get. He shovelled snow and unloaded coal deliveries just as much as he tutored schoolkids. He was able to finish his degree that way, then he worked for two years in the Ruhr district, 'cos he's a mining engineer, and he came back one day at last, it was my darkest time, when I really couldn't see any way out. Everything that meant anything to me back then, parties and nice people, balls, theatres and all the rest, he didn't care about any of that. He just went on his way regardless, and that cured me. I was snippy at first and wanted absolutely nothing to do with him, and that was already a bad sign, because I was interested in him. He told me to my face that I'd get into big trouble. And he gave me solid values and proper standards.

Since then, I've never messed up. He got a job in Soviet Russia a year ago, in the Donetsk Basin, in a coal mine. I write to him all the time. And a letter comes from over there too, now and then, but not very often. I think he'll come back again …'

A name comes into Erna's mind, she immediately regrets having said it: 'Siodmak'.

Erika says nothing for a long time, and Erna doesn't look at her. The hand has slipped off her shoulder.

Erna looks up into the shimmering sky, to the hazy red glow: the lights of the city of Berlin.

'Siodmak? Don't believe all the stories at the office. Take Trude, for example, she said something about Lortzing for the first time today. I was astonished myself. But there's a reason for that. Siodmak's a cunning one, not at all like Lortzing. Lortzing's an employee like everybody else, he does what he's told. But Siodmak's far more dangerous. I used to be afraid of him, now I know him better. Sometimes we go out in his car together. Would you like to come with us one day?'

'No.'

'Up to you. Trude is very sick, and she's looking for something to hold onto, otherwise she'd never be broadcasting her private affairs. The girls try to add two and two and piece things together, because they see a lot and hear even more, and probably you can't hear more gossip anywhere than in an office …'

You can hear the cars, but the noise is muted, as if it's behind a wall, there are gardens and behind the gardens there are streets, the streets of Berlin.

'… and then I get four hundred marks a month, which is more than the usual, I suppose they've already told you all that …'

Erna has become very thoughtful, there are lots of things she doesn't know about yet. Erika is seven years older. Will I have to go through all of that too? she wonders.

'… Georg will come back again one day, and everything will be fine!'

Erna doesn't know how to respond, you've got to work out what's right and what's wrong. This morning Erika was still sarcastic and stand-offish, treating me as if she looked down on me. Now I know that she's good, and strong, she can love, she has good, clear feelings, she was down for the count once, she didn't give up the fight, she's sitting next to me, we're holding hands, we're silent, what an odd evening. A sleepy waiter is rattling around, now they're shutting the doors downstairs, a car is driving out of the garage, a girl with a penetrating voice is singing in the kitchen.

I wish all the people I love were here! Erna is breathing deeply and happily. What a life it is, in this city! She's forgetting a lot.

She takes the train back home, very late at night, right across Berlin.

The next morning, Martha Hummel doesn't turn up to work, and Lieselotte Kries brings a small parcel. That'll be the voile dress, of course. Lieselotte puts the parcel on Erna's little desk without saying anything. Erna looks around casually to see if the other girls have noticed anything. No, even Elsbeth Siewertz is typing industriously. Erna doesn't want to attract attention, she doesn't say anything. But she resolves not to accept the dress under any circumstances, she simply has to speak to Lieselotte about it. When Erna puts the parcel in the cloakroom next to her coat, she sees that there's a letter under the string. Yes, to Fräulein Erna Halbe. It's just a piece of paper with big, round letters swimming around like zeroes.

'I know you'll despise me, but Wolf Tümmler loves me and I love him, and I really didn't want to make any trouble for you. Wolf Tümmler is the only man I truly love.'

And the 'truly' is underlined twice. Erna puts the letter in her pocket.

The days pass, and quite a few things change in the office, slowly but visibly. For example, Elsbeth Siewertz stops in the corridor, astonished, when she sees Erna and Erika immersed in a serious conversation. Then she calls Erna over to her and gives her a felt underlay so that her Orga Privat won't rattle so much. She says this with a serious, dark face, but it's not every girl who can say that Elsbeth gave her a felt underlay.

The girls need Erna's advice here and there, one day little Annemie wanted to find another job, she came to the Orga Privat, and Erna spoke to her very sensibly, Annemie stayed at Iron Processing Co. There are lots of questions to be asked in an office like this, and the answers are often difficult.

Why do the girls come to Erna, in particular? She says things so simply and sensibly, she doesn't make a big fuss, but just listens carefully and then works out something. Well of course, she says, I see it this way, but you must know yourself what you want to do. The girls like that. Mostly they come to her with romantic problems and with lots of other little personal worries.

One morning she straightens out a dispute between Eva and Friedel quite forcefully, and that strengthens her authority considerably.

She's one of the girls now, still the little one at the Orga Privat, but they don't mean anything nasty by it. One morning a Remington comes back from the repair shop, but Erna sticks to her rattly old machine, she's got used to it.

One day, one of the younger stenotypists, a graceful little thing called Grete Theier, comes back crying after taking dictation in Lortzing's room. What's the matter? Lortzing grabbed her and kissed her. Always the same thing. But still, there's something odd about it, Grete's been working in the office for a year and takes dictation from Lortzing all the time, she's never said anything, and suddenly she's in tears. But she's not just crying, she's looking at Erna too.

'What am I supposed to do, when he throws me down into the armchair?'

She's playing the role of Lortzing with great drama.

Erna doesn't have to think for long.

'You should've boxed his ears!'

'Yeah, and I'd have got the sack!'

'No you wouldn't.' Elsbeth takes a hand. 'Do you think we would all have just put up with that?'

'What do you mean?'

The girls gather in a tight circle, some of them are sitting on their desks, they're all listening eagerly.

'If management sacked one of us for something like that, we'd all stop work.'

'Management? What do you mean, management? You're talking about Trude's bosom pal!'

No, that's not funny anymore. Eva Hagedorn climbs onto her desk, she's doing the talking now. Any girl who goes on putting up with something like that is just stupid. We'll simply go on strike, and Lortzing will just be standing there like an idiot. But Eva doesn't really mean it, she's enjoying the commotion, the whole thing is a joke to her.

Erna is very thoughtful all of a sudden. But Elsbeth gets in before her.

'Grete, if you box his ears and he chucks you out, he'll be scared every day that you'll go to his wife. I know that's nasty, but it's how you have to deal with these guys.'

So says Elsbeth Siewertz.

'No.' Erna's shaking her head. 'Don't do anything stupid! If one of us is dismissed and she protests, it'll end up before the Labour Tribunal. And who's going to help us there? Nobody. Elsbeth, do you think that two months' salary as compensation would be any help? No, you'll want a new job, and you won't get one. We'll only get anywhere if we stick together. What I mean is: If Lortzing sees that it's not just Eva or Grete, for example, but it's all of us who won't put up with his tricks, then he'll have to think twice.'

The girls are listening attentively, yes, Erna's right. She's standing among them, serious, sure of herself, she's telling them what they have to do, this stuff is important, and the graceful Grete Theier has started something big. They want to help each other if something happens, they've been putting up with too much for too long, no more! What has got into these girls?

Yes, all kinds of things are changing in this office.

The next morning comes, it's Saturday. The sun is shining into Erna's little room again, a bright, friendly sun. Summer is coming at last. She's not quite fully dressed when there's a knock on the door.

'There's a young lady outside who wants to talk to you.'

Who knows me here? Who climbs up four flights of stairs to speak to little Erna Halbe? Who can it possibly be?

Erna looks in astonishment when Lotte Weissbach walks in with an excited, sweaty face. Lotte looks as if she's been running very fast. She's carrying a newspaper which she hands to Erna without speaking before she comes into the room herself. She points to a small item which is almost invisible under the heading 'Local News':

CHILD ABDUCTED

On Thursday evening, the divorced stenotypist Martha Hummel, 22, resident in Wicleff Street, entered the apartment of her former husband, the businessman Rehbein, during his absence and removed their daughter, 4, custody of whom was

> legally assigned to the father. Hummel has not been seen at her own apartment since. The child's father is offering a reward of 100 marks to any person who can discover the whereabouts of the child or the mother. Relevant information should be provided …

At first the street seems to spin around a little, Erna has to read it again.

'Is that our Martha?'

No doubt about it. What's got into the soft little thing? Just goes there and takes her child. But where can she be now? She can't have any money to live on! Lotte doesn't know.

Does she really not know anything? Lotte is agitated, Erna looks at her thoughtfully.

'You know, a hundred marks isn't much at all. Looks like he's not all that keen to find them.'

'No, and nobody's going to give him any information!'

'So what do you know?'

'Me? What … ? Nothing.'

No, Lotte isn't saying anything. So why did she come running to Erna's apartment first thing in the morning, with the newspaper in her hand?

Now Erna remembers the conversation between Lotte and Martha at the dining hall, but she doesn't ask any more questions, she only says: 'If I knew where Martha was, then we could help her.'

But she's agitated too, like Lotte, and all the other girls when they hear the big news.

Yes, the office doesn't settle down today. Who would've thought that little Martha Hummel would do something like that! She's a little heroine, that's what she is, the girls in the typists' room can be proud of her. Perhaps she's got to earn her living secretly somewhere now, that would be like a story in the movies, oh, if only they knew more about what was going on.

Martha's sister, the thin Elfriede, is sitting on her little chair, completely flabbergasted. She doesn't know what to say. She's so surprised and so shocked that her mind is blank, not a joke, not a word, nothing. She doesn't quite know whether to be angry or proud, so she just looks flabbergasted.

Lortzing comes in at one point, walks through the room, gives one of the girls something to type, checks a carbon copy, but he doesn't notice any of their agitation or concern. All the typewriters in the room are rattling away, the girls are bent over their steno pads, their faces are red, that's because of the work, so what? Lortzing goes out again. There are girls sitting there, right, young stenotypists, right, underpaid, right, but pretty, right, with different faces, exactly ten if you're counting, because one of them is absent and two others have offices elsewhere, none of them is very old, but all of them are very sure of themselves, their hearts are pounding, but you can't hear that. You can only hear their fingers striking the keys and the keys striking the paper.

Child abducted?

They feel like accomplices. Yes, quite a few things are changing in this office.

The week comes to an end, on Sunday they really do go to Werder, work begins again the next day.

There are no further reports about Martha Hummel in the newspapers, it's only a minor case, she's still missing. A police detective does question the employees in the office briefly on Tuesday, yes, but of course nothing comes of it.

No. The girls seem to be pleased that the police haven't discovered anything yet.

Erna is alert when Lotte is called in for questioning. The little red-cheeked girl is extraordinarily pale today, but the detective doesn't notice. Afterwards Lotte looks at all the other girls in turn, nobody pays any attention to her, except that Erna looks at her thoughtfully and reproachfully.

Yes, Erna! Nobody calls her The Girl at the Orga Privat anymore, not even when she isn't there, only Elsbeth uses that kind of nickname sometimes, but then it sounds so gentle and loving that nobody has any objections.

Then it's Wednesday again, Erna has finished her first week, her first week in Berlin.

That evening, she sits in her little room and looks down into the city, which is shrouded in a haze. Night is drawing in quickly. The tired shadows of the spring winds shroud the streets and courtyards in an uncertain light, from which shouts and cries drift up. The last light of day is still straying around up where she's sitting, brushing her cute, little girl's fingers.

What's she holding in her hand? Yes, it's a boy's cap, a flat peaked cap.

Who does this cap belong to? Well, the story isn't a love story, it's quickly told.

This cap belongs to the boy from Koppen Street, she's seen him again.

How small this city of Berlin is after all!

On Sunday evening they were coming back from Werder, pleased with themselves, cheerful, and very tired. They were travelling on the suburban train, Erna was looking out the window. The train had to stop at Lichterfelde for a few minutes. And then a young man is standing on the platform, and just staring at her. She recognizes him, yes, she recognizes him first, and smiles. So now they've run into each other three times, and now her train's about to start again, and he still doesn't know who he's staring at. And then she has to laugh. She's wearing her elegant hat, so she looks very different, but now he does know who she is. The train has started, he's had no chance to say anything, so he takes his cap and throws it through her window. And she catches it. He waves and waves and waves.

And now, three days later, she's sitting in her room looking at the thing. A checked flat cap, nothing more, a kind of greeting. It's a pity, she thinks, that he hasn't collected the cap, 'cos it's a very nice one. But of course he has no way of knowing where Erna lives.

But she knows where he lives.

Of course, the boy has to get his cap back! She puts on her coat and walks to Koppen Street.

But he was about to move out, hmn, what does she do now?

She climbs up all those stairs again, at the top the door is opened by a little fat woman with a sharp face, that'll be Frau Ziegenbein.

'Him! Nah, I threw him out. Where he's living now? No idea. I don't want anything to do with that kind of people …'

Erna couldn't be less interested in Frau Ziegenbein's opinions. But now she does find out the boy's name: Fritz Drehkopf. The police station even has his change-of-residence form, and the little girl who comes asking is told that Fritz Drehkopf is still living in Koppen Street, just a few numbers further on.

He opens the door himself, just like before. He's still rather hairy, and looks taken aback.

'Wow, I've been waiting for you for days.'

'I just wanted to bring you back your cap.'

Of course. She's got to look at his new apartment, and then they talk together for a while, just the kind of things that young people talk about, about the movies and about work and about the city and about love. Actually, they don't talk much about love. And why should they? There's something that's much nicer than talking about it.

Who is this girl? She's only seen him three times before, only for a few minutes, but still she knows for sure that he's a nice, honest guy. Being his friend is worth it.

That night, she sleeps with him.

He gets out of bed bright and early in the morning, because he has to go to work earlier than Erna does.

She's still there among the pillows, a bit tired, and with a fresh, happy face. Her eyes are very big, and they follow everything Fritz does, how he washes, dresses, and then makes his own coffee. And in between times he comes over and puts his arms around her so tightly she can hardly breathe.

'Hey, another time I'll make coffee for you. But today you'll have to make some for yourself, I'm still so tired!'

He shaves in front of a little mirror on the wall, watching her as he does so. He's thinking about how lovely she is. He makes a sort of list of her beauty. She has wonderfully soft hair and a classic nose, not an insignificant little thing like all the other girls have. She doesn't need to colour her moist lips, they're naturally full and red and shining. And she's got a wonderful body, too, strong, well-formed and a little bit plump, just the way he likes it.

When he's finished dressing, she gets out of bed too.

And such beautiful legs. He turns around to admire them. Slim and straight, like a little boy's, he says.

She thinks they're a bit knock-kneed. That's just what he likes, he says. He wants to look at them more closely. No, she stamps her feet and overextends her legs and bursts into tears like a little kid. Then he grabs her tightly, around her back and the backs of her knees, and waltzes around the room with her, because she won't put up with that, she's strong and has good bones.

It's only when she crawls back into bed, pulled about and exhausted, with rubbery legs and tousled hair, that he stops.

Then they drink coffee together, and he butters some big rolls for her good and thick. She's hungry, her big white teeth tear into the bread, since Monday she hasn't been able to eat anything except lunch, because she spent the last of her money in Werder, and that wasn't much to start with. All she's got left now is some meals on the multiticket for the dining hall.

She knows that won't be enough, hunger is tough, already when she's typing away sometimes her vision starts to flicker, that's why she answered a newspaper advertisement from a packaging company to write addresses in her spare time. There are a few packets of envelopes and an address list on her table at home, she's already done seventy. You can't earn much, one pfennig per address, but she'll be able to buy a bit more to eat.

They've finished their delicious breakfast.

'I liked you right away', he says, 'when you wanted to rent the room at Frau Ziegenbein's, but you wouldn't let me get a word in. You've got no idea how unremarkable you looked. I thought to myself: There's something to be made of that girl.'

He says that with as much amiable condescension as if he'd bought her the new hat and the new dress, and cut her fringe himself.

She walks with Fritz to the auto-repair workshop where he's employed as a mechanic. Fritz and Erna say goodbye at the gate, and lots of people are walking past that gate. They embrace in front of everybody, and kiss. And then she waves until she can't see him anymore.

A few workers say things to her, she walks past with a proud, amiable expression. Young girls follow her with their eyes and laugh.

The sky above the city is promising a good day, the streets are steaming with warmth, it's as if she's running through a glittering sea, the air is shimmering.

Crowds of girls in light, bright-coloured dresses are walking into the offices and department stores and shops.

I'll alter Lieselotte's voile dress today, Erna decides.

Isn't everything turning out for her? Isn't she happy to be living in the city of Berlin? And then she has to think about Trude. She can see that the girl is getting sicker and sicker, she knows that something will have to be done for her, but Trude just won't talk about it. She acts as if absolutely nothing happened in the dining hall at Alexander Square. Trude has forgotten her promise. She's giving no details, she's saying nothing, she's keeping to herself. And Erna knows that if she asks, she won't get an answer. She's afraid for Trude.

And on this beautiful morning, she has to think about that.

And now she's supposed to be doing those envelopes every evening, writing addresses. This beautiful morning makes her wonder if she'll stick to it.

She gets to the office early. There are only a few girls sitting in the typists' room.

Vera Kränkel, one of the younger ones, with black hair and blue eyes, is waving around a love letter which she got from somebody unknown, Lotte Weissbach is commenting on it in her funny way, the girls have to laugh.

Trude is already there too. She has pursed her little heart-shaped mouth as if to whistle and is painting it, guiding the lipstick with the little finger of her left hand.

Erna looks at her closely.

'How are you?'

Trude looks up out of her astonishingly bright eyes, and keeps dabbing the lipstick.

'Well.'

That's a lie, her lips are bloodless, there are heavy dark shadows under her eyes.

It's eight o'clock, all the girls are there.

Little, determined Otti has a bunch of simple meadow flowers in a water glass next to her typewriter.

'Who are they from?' Eva asks. 'Your milk-cart driver, or the delivery-truck guy?'

'If you want flowers, your loving husband can give you some', Otti drawls.

'Hey, I wouldn't put weeds like that on my desk.'

Otti doesn't worry about the chatter, she was brought up in Wedding, where the workers live, and the girls don't collect admirers. But her boys love her.

The morning passes slowly, the girls type languidly and tiredly, the letters they tap out monotonously hour after hour, day after day, dance in front of their eyes. The early warmth weighs heavily on their young limbs. They're all still tired from the evening before, some of them danced all night, the others darned stockings and fixed up dresses, and Erna was with Fritz Drehkopf. They all have to get through a certain allocation of work, and it's not a small one. The bosses check everything carefully, anybody who falls behind is simply dismissed.

Trude is hardly working at all now, her handkerchief is pressed to her mouth, she props her head on her hand and doesn't talk to anybody, she seems to be really sick. But Erna, who's watching her, doesn't realize how far it's gone. Shortly before twelve, Trude Leussner collapses. She has to vomit again. Erna takes her out.

Outside, Trude starts wailing, she's retching violently and trembling. Erna pats her on the back, she doesn't quite know why, she just wants to comfort Trude and find out for sure what's wrong with the girl. She doesn't beat about the bush anymore.

'Listen, have you had a procedure?'

And then everything comes out.

Yes, Trude had a bust-up with Lortzing, because he didn't want anything to do with it. She's known for three months. First she couldn't believe it, then she was so afraid she tried all kinds of things, potions and turpentine and some disgusting herbal stuff and then injections.

'Lortzing gave me the money, but I couldn't find a doctor who would do it.' Erna looks seriously at this naïve twenty-year-old girl, she knows the score better than anybody here.

'Why didn't you say something to me before? But you mustn't try anything else now, understood? Nothing! Nothing at all! I'll try to find a doctor somewhere.' And when Trude begins sobbing again, she adds: 'Come on, calm down, you'll get better again. Does it hurt?'

'Yes.'

Trude has stabbing pains in her abdomen, and she feels like something is bleeding somewhere.

Erna gives her some water to drink.

'I'd advise you to go home.'

No, Trude doesn't want to do that, her mother always looks at her so oddly, she simply refuses to go home.

There's a terrible smell in the washroom, Erna opens a window, because Trude wants to rest here for a bit longer.

Everything in the washroom is silent, except for a tap which is dripping with a hollow sound. Trude stands there with her head bent forward, Erna watches her.

After a while they go out.

Lortzing is standing in the corridor, he looks as if he's just let go of the door handle, he's blocking their way.

Erna looks at him carefully, she's quite calm, the man can't bother her anymore. He's stroking his clean-shaven chin.

'Fräulein Leussner, you know that things can't go on like this. After all, you're doing hardly any work. If you're going to be sick all the time, you'll just have to find a position which is more suited to your health.'

For a moment, Erna is speechless with fury, she can't say anything at all, she'd like to punch him. But before she can find the right words Trude, the classy Trude, spits on Herr von Lortzing's shoes and walks away.

All Lortzing can say is: 'That's going much too far.'

He disappears hastily into his room.

In the corridor everything is quiet, the girls are all waiting in the typists' room, most of them with their hats and coats on, because it's already one o'clock.

'So what did Lortzing want from you?'

'Did you see him?'

'Yes, he went into the washroom.'

So that's how it is, Erna thinks to herself, he heard everything that Trude told me. Well, that can't hurt. Quite the opposite. There's no way that Lortzing will get out of this business unscathed.

Erna wants to use this lunchbreak to find a doctor who can sort out this kind of thing. She gets Erika Tümmler to give her a medical insurance certificate for Trude, and sets off.

Of course, she doesn't know any addresses here in Berlin, she doesn't know anything, but Trude has got to be helped.

It's a difficult journey. She hopes that the quickest way to find a doctor will be in the area around Frankfurt Avenue. She can see all the white plaques on the buildings from a long way off, and then she walks up the staircases and down the staircases. She tells the same story over and over again. Her sister is three months pregnant, and now the engagement has gone sour, can something be done? The responses vary between regretful shoulder-shrugging, polite negation and brusque dismissal.

All these indifferent faces are making Erna afraid, and she's getting tired. Trude Leussner has got to be examined by a doctor right away, and nobody wants to help. She feels as if she is sick herself, and is running for her life now.

Soon she finds herself out in Rummelsburg, there aren't as many streets, it seems that no doctors live here. But then she does find a plaque on a new corner building and climbs up three floors. A female doctor is living there, in two very small rooms. There are no patients waiting, Erna is sent in immediately – or rather the doctor, a tall lady of about thirty-five, opens the door herself. She looks fresh and very healthy, probably people take her for younger than she really is, her open face inspires confidence.

Erna, who feels somewhat helpless and flat after all the walking, and despairing after her hopeless search, leans against the wall to rest for a moment. She hasn't had any lunch either. Her lips whisper inaudibly: You have to help … I won't leave until … until I'm sure that Trude will be allowed to come here.

'Come in', the doctor says. 'Are you very tired? What seems to be the trouble?'

Her voice is hard, she speaks impersonally, professionally.

So Erna doesn't lie, she doesn't make up a little story, she tells everything exactly as it really happened, the whole grubby office affair between Trude and Herr von Lortzing.

The whitewashed room is uncomfortably warm, a single fly is buzzing somewhere. Oppressive silence, frightening silence and the smell of carbolic.

The sky outside is blue, there's just one cloud sailing across it.

The sky looks hopeless.

Erna can see out the window, to the land which hasn't been built on. It's a mixture of allotment gardens and garbage dumps, with a sprinkling of junkyards and things like that in between. A factory chimney is emitting a thin stream of smoke which doesn't fit in with the blue of the sky at all, and smears it.

We never forget hours like these, they return, desolate, tired, sad, frightening …

Erna chokes out her story in an uncertain voice, she has difficulty holding back her tears, suddenly she feels as if a great deal depends on Trude getting well again …

The doctor is sitting on a smooth white wooden chair, turned in Erna's direction, with her legs crossed. Her white coat has fallen to the side, Erna sees the beautiful strong legs and the firm hands resting on the lap. The doctor's even-tempered face doesn't change for a moment. She's wearing a slim silver band in her chestnut-brown hair.

'But why hasn't your friend come herself ?'

Because … And because …

'And why did you come to me, in particular? Did somebody send you?'

Erna tells her how she's been running from one doctor to another, one disappointment to another.

'Yes, my dear child, it's a difficult business. Of course, taking precautions is always better than trying to cure things after the fact.'

Erna knows that, she tells Trude's story. She defends Trude. A twenty-year-old girl, she says, who sees nice things all around her, and whose girlfriends are having a good time and who can't get married in the foreseeable future, is she supposed to just sit around and wait, with her hundred and thirty marks? …

The doctor waves her hand, she knows that. And she'd very much like to help, but of course it isn't so easy. She says that Erna should leave her address, she will definitely hear something.

That's some hope at least, a small hope, all this difficult midday journey wasn't in vain.

Hungry, dusty and tired, Erna gets back to the office twenty minutes late. She goes straight to Trude.

'Right, no need to be worried, we'll help you. I found something!'

Trude looks up gratefully, there are big dark shadows under her eyes, her face is tired and pinched.

'It still hurts.'

She points to her abdomen.

'Surely Lortzing has said or done something … ? No? I'm surprised.'

'Ach, no reason to be afraid because of that. He just wanted to play the tough guy. But there's no chance he'll chuck me out. He wouldn't dare.'

Everything in the typists' room is in a mess, there was a squabble about the work allocations. Some of the girls proclaimed that they had been given far too much, Lieselotte is still carrying on about it.

There are piles of records and reports on Erna's desk which she has to type. And she's so tired from chasing around the city!

The typewriter with its forty-five keys is staring at this little girl's strong hands: cold, hostile, and completely unconcerned. Her touchingly firm and industrious fingers tap out their monotonous rhythm, touch-typing, hands based over the correct keys. Her joints are hurting, and there's a twinge in her lower arm, and her head aches … a, s, d, f … j, k, l, ö … Thumbs on the space bar … that's how she learned to touch-type …

'The Wetzlar-Gräser electric welding process …'

The letters dance up and down, outside spring is going at full blast, rowing regatta on Müggel Lake …

And just where has Martha Hummel taken herself off to? Ah, Erna knows something, but she's not saying anything yet. She'll wait. Somebody will come to her eventually and ask her advice.

The typewriters clack away.

Grete Theier, in a bilious green chiffon dress, sits down at Erna's desk. Erna listens as she types. At first little Grete talks about trivialities …

'… so now I'm having a suit made from yellow Panama-weave fabric, with a white blouse and a bow at the top. Light and pleated, like Elsbeth's one …'

Elsbeth always wears tasteful clothes, modern and chic, you can't deny that.

But Grete Theier has other things to worry about.

'… I can't stand the yammering and the endless you-shouldn'ting at my parents' place anymore. If I'm not home by midnight, it's the end of the world. Nothing I do is right, they always find something to criticize me for. I really don't need to put up with that anymore. And my clothes are never where they're supposed to be, or they haven't even been washed by the time I want them, and sometimes they're so creased that there's just no point putting them on. My lovely lace underwear – I had so much of it – was ruined in the wash. There's almost none of it left now …'

'Well, if you move out you'll have to do all of that yourself, and other things as well.'

'Yes, I know that, but if you're living on your own it's not all as difficult as it is at home, where you assume that things will be done properly. The only good thing at home is that I can eat as much as I like. I'm giving them eighty marks, and of course that's not enough to live on in your own place …'

'Even a hundred and twenty marks wouldn't be enough!'

Grete earns the same as Erna does at Iron Processing Co., one hundred and thirty marks gross per month, but her friend, Herr Einsiedel, would pay for her to have her own apartment, then she would only have to pay for her food herself …

'I don't know your Herr Einsiedel.'

'You know, he's a chief clerk in the Darmstadt and National Bank. No, no, he's not married, he really loves me. And I really like him. He's a little over forty, but that doesn't matter, he still looks very imposing, and I don't go with the young idiots anyway, they're no fun. We've known each other for at least six months now, we go out every evening, so it's all legitimate. And I haven't told anybody about it yet, you're the first …'

Erna knows exactly what's true here and what isn't. Elsbeth and Erika, at least, know this Herr Einsiedel as well.

'… sometimes we go to see a show at the Scala or the Winter Garden, or to one of the theatres, and we go to the movies a lot. He knows all the good cabarets, and he's a fabulous dancer. I mean, you wouldn't think it to look at him, but really it's true! He's funny and nice, you should come out with us sometime. He's always very polite and obliging to me, and if you knew how concerned he is about me you'd die laughing. He dances to my tune alright! And then he's a really decent guy! I can't complain. You know, if my parents weren't so damned suspicious I'd take him home to meet them sometime. He earns a lot, he'd have no trouble paying for an apartment for me. I've looked at it from all the angles. I'll just tell my parents that I'd got a pay rise. Pay attention, Erna, let's work it out, I'm seventeen now …'

Yes, Grete Theier is eighteen months younger than Erna, but she looks older. Although if you look just at her doll's face, the round and expressionless porcelain eyes, the carefully arranged curls, the little nose, the two dimples in her gently glowing little cheeks, everything in a kind of miniature version, then you'd like to pick her up and coo over her like a baby. But as soon as she leaves the typists' room and is dressed for the street, she becomes a great lady you wouldn't dare to approach. She always wears a big fur coat, partnered with an elegant black hat with a half-veil. She trips along the street, taking short steps in tiny, close-fitting shoes. The men watch her intently. Young people follow her longingly with their eyes, without the least idea of her underpaid stenotypist's life at Iron Processing Co. She looks so expensive and delicate that even Erna, the calm and resolute Erna, feels an odd desire to take her in her arms and kiss her. She particularly likes the fact that Grete isn't really arrogant at all. Little Grete knows exactly what she's worth, and she wears elegant clothes because people admire her, and because Herr Einsiedel pays for her beautiful, expensive things.

So on this late afternoon, sitting at Erna's desk, Grete Theier talks simply and clearly about her little affairs without trying to be superior. What she wants from Erna is some simple, straightforward advice, or perhaps just approval for a decision which she's been too nervous to carry out yet. She loves Erna. Erna discusses everything seriously with her and doesn't rush off to tell everybody else …

While Grete is describing Herr Einsiedel's virtues, her right arm wanders around in the air for a bit before landing gently on Erna's shoulders. Erna squints at it in surprise. But it does her good.

Then Lortzing comes in, the girls have to work faster, there's a big backlog.

In the evening, young men are standing on the other side of Prenzlau Avenue, waiting. And there's an automobile, or more accurately two, the right one and the wrong one. The wrong one is the delivery truck where a young man in corduroy trousers is adjusting the number two seat. The girls already know who's going to sit there.

The boy turns around, he's heard somebody calling out, Otti runs into his arms and takes his hands. They climb on (Otti swings herself up quickly and elegantly) and chug off.

Erna watches them with mixed feelings. That Ottilie doesn't come out of her shell as quickly as the other girls do, she does her work quietly by herself, not worrying much about her colleagues' business. After work she climbs onto the back of the delivery truck and takes off with her boyfriend without giving a damn about what people think. They're getting married soon.

Even Herr Kries, jovial and a little odd as always, has put in an appearance today, and Lieselotte feels compelled to greet him extravagantly on the street with a kiss.

But Fritz Drehkopf is nowhere to be seen, even though he'd promised that morning that he'd pick Erna up. And Erna had been so looking forward to seeing the expressions on the other girls' faces when they saw their Erna Halbe together with a nice young man.

She walks up and down for a bit, waiting.

Only when the girls have disappeared and the employees in the building at the front, who work a little later, are finishing up, does she see him walking towards her slowly. That's odd, he's coming from the opposite direction, his repair shop isn't that way.

Erna runs impatiently to meet him.

He has dressed up, she examines the pressed blue suit and brightly spotted tie with astonishment. And he's wearing a soft hat too. Everything looks a bit too classy for the mechanic Fritz Drehkopf.

Erna looks at him with a question in her eyes. His good-natured boyish face is clouded visibly by anger.

'Chucked out', he says.

Erna is shocked.

'If you knew how furious I am … Well, come on, it's not your fault. I mean, the old man always disliked me, because I told him to his face every time he messed something up. Herr Doctor of Engineering thinks he knows everything, but he hasn't got a clue. So we get a nice car this morning, it won't go. Well, we have a look, something wrong with the magneto. He starts fiddling around with the spark plugs. Stop that, I said. So he raps my fingers with a spanner. I punched him. He couldn't breathe properly for a good five minutes. That was worth it. Dismissed without notice, right. I go to the office, want to get my money. I mean, they owe me for six days. They wouldn't give me my money or my papers. You know, it doesn't matter that I got the sack, I'll get another job alright. Or we'll just have to live on the unemployment pay for a week. But trying to hang onto my money and my papers, which I'm entitled to by law, that'll cost them. I'll start by getting my money tomorrow morning. You can count on it ...'

They're walking down Lothringen Street towards Invaliden Street, quite aimlessly. Erna has put her arm through Fritz's, they're very close together as they stroll, she says nothing at all, and his fury ebbs away. He even becomes apologetic: 'Had to wait a long time, didn't you? Couldn't get there any earlier, this got in the way, and I had to change my clothes. You can count on it, little girl, I'm always punctual!'

The warm evening air flows across the city, the city which is still working, and won't rest for a long time yet. You can hear music from a shop that sells radios. A wonderful female voice is singing her part in a duet from Verdi's *Troubadour*. Lots of people are listening, lost in the music. And they're waiting for the tram too, because there's a stop outside the radio shop. A bit further on, they come to an express restaurant. Fritz Drehkopf once had a bit of a thing going with the flaxen-haired girl who sells the hot sausages. But she was too snippy and had exaggerated ambitions; still, their parting was completely amicable. Fritz can still remember the girl's glittering nail polish and her penetrating voice. He walks quickly past the restaurant without looking in. Erna is holding on tight to his arm, she pushes her right hand into his, her hand feels warm and soft, its pressure says: I'm not letting go of you again.

They're not really talking very much, Fritz looks down at the little girl who's so nice and graceful and young as she walks beside him. He decides that he's never had such a pretty girl, and that puts him in a good mood again.

When they get to Lehrte Station, Fritz stops suddenly and pulls her into a doorway. He looks at her importantly and takes out his wallet and a little green cloth bag with coins and counts his money.

'Look out!' he says, 'now we'll go to see the most beautiful thing in Berlin!'

'What are you talking about?'

He grabs her hands, they walk over to the station, and take the train to Luna Park.

Just opened! Everything still smells a little of renovation and 'Caution! Wet Paint!' But the atmosphere is just right for Berlin, crowds of people are streaming in. There are colourful lanterns hanging there, they're probably lit at dusk. Erna's happy, this is going to be a fun evening! She doesn't want anything in particular, her boyfriend isn't supposed to spend any money, he hasn't got much, after all. She just wants to walk along beside him, through the warm spring evening, past all the happy people, get away from the sad things and the tormenting things. She wants to be happy, happy, very happy …

But Fritz has a serious face. No, he knows the right thing to do. He wants to show his girl Luna Park, and of course he's going to pay for her. He has to drag the reluctant Erna onto the carousel with the swinging chairs, she clings on desperately up there. She's afraid of the buzzing feeling in her stomach. And then they're off … Fritz grabs the chain on her swing with his hand and pushes Erna a long way out as they go round and round. The people below her are moving in circles, as is the sky above her, one runs into the other, the colours get all swirled up together, she has to roar with laughter. Fritz catches her and pushes her a long way out again and again. Then they take a ride on the roller coaster, screech with laughter on the wobbling staircase, slide around in the bumper cars, look at a variety stage with Lilliputians and a really lovely trapeze act, they shoot at things and throw things, and Erna wins a portion of eel which she eats on the spot. They don't have any money left for the dance pavilions, but they don't actually need any. They dance outside, to the muted sound of the music from the expensive restaurants and bars, they hold each other close throughout the darkening night. They can feel their hearts and their arms and their thighs and their legs. They walk through the streets of Luna Park, laughing, cheerful, happy, nibble chocolate, kiss each other thoroughly and – incidentally – they don't think about how Fritz has blown his last eight marks. And why should they think about that?

Erna holds onto the back of her boyfriend's neck, he's a bit big for her, but she's happy. They go home very late.

'Come back to my place!' Erna says, drawing his face down to her mouth.

In the train, she tells him the story with Trude and Lortzing and what's happening in the company. He listens seriously and attentively.

'Listen', he says, 'that's a difficult business. They definitely won't be pleased. Of course, you girls mustn't take a backward step. Most office workers are shit, but there's always a first time. Do you know the other boss, what was his name again?'

'Lortzing?'

'Nah, I meant the other one.'

'He's called Siodmak. Erika Tümmler is his girlfriend.'

'Do you know him any better?'

'We hardly ever see him. I had to report to him on the first day, he was very nice then. But that's all I know.'

'Don't let them fool you. If something new happens, you've got to tell me about it at once. Then I'll tell you what you've got to do. Are any of you in a union, maybe?'

Erna doesn't know, she used to belong to the Central Association of Office Workers, but then she left.

'That's a pity', Fritz says thoughtfully, 'do you think that the girls might – I mean, if one of you gets chucked out or if they cut your salaries – that they'd do something then ... ? You know, resist in some way ...'

'Yes', Erna says, 'that kind of thing is always hard to predict, and I don't know the girls very well yet either. They're ambitious and want to earn lots of money, well, we want to do that too, but they think they're a cut above the workers. Not all of them, Otti's different, and maybe a few others. But I don't think they'd do anything if the bosses acted against them. They don't have the courage for it, or the pride and ... well, I don't know how to put it ...'

'No class consciousness', Fritz says.

'No, they haven't got that. You know, I think they've been changing a bit recently. When they see that there are more things than pretty clothes and rich admirers and things like that. Yes, I don't know, I think I could probably do something with them …'

The train bumps on from station to station through the night. The two young people are sitting close together. His big, chapped mechanic's paws are lying on her lap, she strokes them gently.

The next morning, the rain is drumming on the windowsills. They get dressed. Erna is worried about Frau Matschek, of course she mustn't see hide nor hair of Fritz.

'It'd be best if you slipped out now, before she brings the coffee.'

Of course, when they open the door cautiously Frau Matschek is standing in the hallway with an angry, poisonous look on her face and her head bent down. It looks like she's been there quite a while, listening and waiting.

Erna stammers: 'Good morning!'

'Please clear out the room immediately, I don't need that kind of lodgers.' And she sails away in her dirty, threadbare housecoat before the pair, who are standing there stunned, can say anything. Fritz Drehkopf is the first to get a grip on himself.

'Old bag!' he calls after her.

Frau Matschek's door bangs shut.

These two of God's children look at each other. Erna can still feel the shock in her stomach. Haggard old Matschek looked quite puffed up and anaemic while she was lurking there.

But Fritz grabs his girl by the shoulders and spins her around in the hallway, the apartment echoing with his laughter.

'Hey, aren't you happy to get out of this dump?'

She nods without understanding him.

'Pay attention now!' he says loudly and threateningly. It's certain that his voice can be heard throughout the apartment. If anybody was listening behind the kitchen door, they could make out every word.

'You paid for the whole month, right?' he roars.

Erna nods. Yes, Fritz is a smart guy. It's good that she has him around.

'The old girl can't just chuck you out, she has to give you the legal notice.'

The apartment is still echoing.

'But we'll make an exception this evening, you understand?' he bellows, 'we'll leave this noble virgin lady this evening, assuming that the remainder of your rent is sitting nicely on the table here.'

There's a little garden table in the entryway.

Erna looks at it confusedly and asks shyly: 'Why?'

'Because', he laughs out loud, 'we'll be locking your room.'

And that's what they do.

Making a great noise and commotion, they leave.

'Ugh', Fritz says, in a noticeably softer tone of voice as they walk down the stairs, 'now we've both been more or less cast out of home! We really have bad luck with our landladies. Well, of course, you can stay at my place for the moment, then we'll look for something suitable.'

Vehicles and people glide through the veils of rain, blurred like shadows. Fritz takes his girlfriend to the office; he has time, after all. They walk beside each other like good comrades, matching their steps. They arrange to meet that evening at half-past six, at Aschinger's in Alexander Square.

The building is completely quiet.

Lotte Weissbach is standing at the door of the typists' room.

'Come on in.'

Oh, what can have happened this time?

Lotte points to Trude Leussner's desk, which has a letter on it, an interoffice communication on a sheet of blue paper.

The girls are sitting on their chairs around the desk, looking at Erna. They aren't all there yet. And Trude isn't.

Erna holds up the letter: an interoffice communication on a sheet of blue paper, folded and sealed at one end. It's embossed with 'Iron Processing Co.', and addressed 'To Fräulein Gertrud Leussner, Internal'.

The girls look at Erna expectantly. She takes off her coat first.

While she's doing so, Elsbeth Siewertz appears, and is given the news.

Hmn, she tries to slit open the paper with her thumbnail.

'That'll be her dismissal.'

Of course, the others know that, they don't need Elsbeth to tell them.

'Leave it', Erna says, 'does anybody know where Trude is?'

No, how should the girls know that? And who knows if the letter really is Trude's notice?

They're all waiting until she comes.

Eight o'clock.

The girls start typing.

The letter is lying on the empty desk, blue, solitary, dangerous. Trude doesn't come.

'Yes', Erna begins, 'Elsbeth is probably right. And if it really is her notice, what are you going to do then?'

The girls are confused, Erna is speaking so calmly and seriously, there's no possibility that she's joking. Didn't they promise to stand up for each other? Don't they want to show Lortzing and Siodmak that they're not obliged to spend their lives typing for Iron Processing Co. … ?

'Oh yes you are, that's the point, you are obliged to, you depend on the pittance that you earn here …'

'So we're supposed to just stand by and watch while Trude gets chucked out?' Elsbeth calls out angrily.

The girls are horrified, they want to give Lortzing something to think about, and now Erna, of all people, is backing down …

'No, I'm just telling you that we can't fight the battle the way you're all thinking. We have to do it in a way which makes it impossible for them to chuck us out. Wait, Elsbeth, let me finish. We'll use the only possible tactic at our disposal: We'll stop work …'

The girls squeal and clap. Yes, they'll go on strike, and mess up this joint. Eva has already jammed the F-key on her typewriter …

'But it's not as simple as you all think. Firstly, you mustn't give them any kind of cause for complaint. You've got to keep doing your work properly and as usual, yes, you have no idea what's in the letter. But if they really do want to chuck Trude out, then we'll fight right enough, and then each of you has to understand that we've got to see it through and we mustn't give in. Are any of you in a union?'

The girls look at each other in surprise, why is she asking that?

'Nobody, then', Erna says.

Then a high, scratchy voice is heard, Annemie Bergemann, one of the little flappers like Vera Kränkel and Grete Theier, says that she's in the German Clerks' Association.

What's that?

Her membership card is at home.

'Right. One, at least. Bring in the card next time.'

'But I haven't paid the dues in ages and ages!'

'Never mind, bring in the card.'

Elfriede Hummel remembers something suddenly. Her sister Martha is in the Central Association of Office Workers. Of course it had to be Martha, who isn't here.

'Hello!' Elsbeth calls out.

Trude is standing in the doorway. She looks even paler than usual.

'The pain is terrible again', she says apologetically.

She takes off her hat and coat.

Why are the girls so quiet, why isn't anybody typing, why is everybody looking in her direction?

She turns around, Erna points to the letter.

Trude's mouth narrows in anger, she walks quickly to her desk, tears open the letter and reads, she understands. Notice for the first of next month. For inadequate work.

'Ach, that's a new one', Erna says, 'for inadequate work!'

Trude receives the news with a surprising lack of emotion, it looks like she was expecting it; she's much more worried about the pain.

The girls come to her desk, one after the other, and say something.

They won't chuck you out, we'll stick together, we'll help you, things like that. Trude has to smile, and that's probably Erna's doing.

'So has anybody seen Siodmak? Or Lortzing? No?'

Erika Tümmler apparently has no idea that Trude Leussner has received her notice either, she usually goes straight to her room in the morning, and she hasn't come over yet today.

'Erika? Don't rely on her! She'll leave you all in the lurch for sure, she would have had to type Trude's letter.'

'How do you know that?' Erna looks over at Elfriede Hummel, furious. 'I mean, you don't know Erika at all.'

'Longer than you, any day.'

That can't be denied.

But …

Erika Tümmler brings in some work to be typed.

Erna tells her the story with Trude.

Erika knows nothing about it.

'Listen, Erika, we've already talked about it, we've simply got to make them take the notice back.'

'I'm with you', is all Erika says.

Aha, Erika is with us? The girls look at each other in astonishment. So things are getting serious now. For a moment, all the bitter things which have happened to them here crowd into their minds. Being yelled at, punished, made to do work over; bullying, discourtesy, insults, deductions from their pay. Of course, the way they feel and react is different depending on their personality and how brave they are and how much they understand, some of them have a backbone, others have only been carried along, and standing in the middle of it all is this little girl who types on a wobbly Orga Privat.

At Erna's suggestion, they set up an action committee. Erika, Erna, Lotte Weissbach and Elsbeth are elected unanimously.

Nobody suggests Trude Leussner, she's sitting apathetically behind her desk.

The action committee is to devise a plan. At lunchtime today.

Suddenly Trude Leussner collapses again, but it's worse this time. She slides under her desk without making a sound, her face is distorted, her white teeth are shining in her open mouth.

Otti squats down next to where Trude is lying in a heap and looks at Erna. Her face is set.

'Unconscious', she says.

Yes, Erna must act now. There's a doctor's office diagonally across the street from the typists' room, he should come over immediately.

Lieselotte Kries rushes off, and promptly returns with a youngish, reserved gentleman who looks briefly at Trude and then says one word: 'Hospital'.

A quarter-hour later there are only nine girls left sitting in the office.

And then the typists' room transforms itself imperceptibly into a battlefield. Although the girls don't attribute any particularly worrying significance to Trude's removal, it's causing a lot of unrest and tension.

The rain fades away, with only some individual heavy drops still splashing onto the fresh-smelling, steaming earth. Iron Processing Co. doesn't realize that a storm is brewing on its own premises. Nine girls in the typists' room and two girls in the private offices are hammering away on their typewriters. It's early, on a rainy day in May, the calendar says that it's Friday.

Erna's cheeks are warm with pleasure. When she looks around the room, and sees the girls completing the work assigned to them without looking up, she sits tall in her chair. She's proud, proud of the girls and proud of herself. The hours pass quickly for her.

The dining hall on Alexander Square becomes their headquarters. Today the girls from Iron Processing Co. don't sit in the middle of the room where everybody can see them, as they usually do.

No. Today they need somewhere quieter. Erna goes over to the battered green sofa in the corner at the back, next to the corridor leading to the washroom.

The four can sit undisturbed there, and Erna speaks. She says, we have to present an ultimatum, and it has to be so firm as to leave absolutely no room for negotiation. She says, we can't just demand Trude's reinstatement, that's only half the battle. We have to advance at the same time. All of you except for Erika are underpaid, less than you're legally entitled to. We'll demand what we're legally entitled to. And if our ultimatum isn't accepted, then it won't be a strike, but something else, I don't know the right word, Erika said it to me, I can't remember ...

'Passive resistance', Erika says.

'... yes, and you see that's something different, we can't just call a strike and then go home and go to bed. Lortzing will phone the Labour Office, and thirteen new girls will be typing away at Iron Processing Co. No, we've got to stay in the typists' room, but we mustn't lift a finger to do any work. If we're called to take dictation, we'll stay where we are. If the phone rings in Lotte's office, then she won't put the call through. We'll put the covers on the typewriters and wait, and in the meantime the gentlemen can just think about whether they want to give in or not ...'

That's roughly what Erna says.

Her work colleagues listen attentively, all of this is new to them. What Erna is saying to them so calmly and assuredly seems daring and dangerous, the girls have taken a step forward, they can't really go back anymore.

Erna would make any deserter contemptible in an instant.

Erika, Elsbeth and Lotte of the action committee agree to this plan. But will all the girls stick it out? That question is already hovering above the battle as it's being prepared.

Erika and Elsbeth go back when the discussion is concluded, Erna and Lotte stay and drink a bottle of mineral water together. Hilde, the redhead, is sitting at a nearby table again, she gives them a friendly wave.

Lotte is thinking feverishly about how lonely her office will be this afternoon, when she's not putting the phone calls through. And she's thinking about something else too …

'By the way, my landlady has given me my notice', Erna is telling her. 'Yes, chucked me out. Because Fritz stayed the night … No, this morning …'

'Ach.'

'I'll have to stay with Fritz tonight.'

'Oh, no, don't you want to move in with us?'

Erna turns around, beaming all over her face.

'With you? With you and Martha Hummel?'

But Lotte isn't at all surprised, she just has a worried expression.

'Yes, yes, I know that you worked it out. And it's probably better that way. And Martha wanted me to tell you too. But I'm careful about that kind of thing. Which of the chatterboxes do you trust, anyway? I'll tell you something, my heart is pounding. And now the girl thinks it's a good idea to laugh! Yes, I feel as if I'd committed all kinds of crimes. You know, perhaps it's all to the good that the old woman threw you out. You can bring all your stuff to us this evening, your Fritz will be able to help, and then we'll all live together. You don't know my landlady yet, she'll go along with all of it.'

Yes, Erna thinks that's a good idea.

'How's Martha's daughter doing?'

'She always has to stay upstairs in the apartment because Martha doesn't want to show herself on the street too often, and of course that's annoying. But maybe she'll go to her aunt's place in Bavaria next week, they've got a little farm there. Of course, I'd gone through everything with her and made preparations long ago, and once Martha decides to do something, she always sees it through ... No, her husband doesn't seem to be trying particularly hard to find her. Anyway, there's not a soul who has an inkling of how and where. Only Frau Pratt, that's my landlady, she's a treasure, I'm telling you, she knows the score and she's helping whenever she can.'

Lotte's cheeks are glowing, she's fired up by the battle, she's forgotten her boyfriend, she phones him every day to put him off, she's forgotten that she's twenty years old, she's almost forgotten that her heart is pounding, now she can see an objective, and behind that another objective is coming into view, and she can see the sky above it, still clouded with rain today, lit by the sun tomorrow ... an objective, a good, clear objective!

The battle commences.

Erna types a nice clean copy of the ultimatum on her Orga Privat. The girls are all standing expectantly around her desk. It's funny, one or another of them changed her clothes at lunchtime. They've got good going-out clothes on, it's funny.

Lotte and Erika stay in the typists' room too, that's what they arranged. An unusual, expectant and solemn calm is pressing down on all of them.

The calm before the storm? Erna observes the girls. Are any of them afraid already? she wonders.

But before the girls get the chance to send their demands to Lortzing and Siodmak, the business seems to come to a head. Because Herr Lortzing appears in the typists' room, angry, yapping, discourteous. The girls rush to their chairs as if nothing's going on here.

Only Erika and Erna remain standing.

Lortzing is completely taken aback by what he sees, and doesn't know which act of rudeness or sloppiness he should complain about first.

'Fräulein Weissbach! The telephone has been ringing enough to wake the dead, and you're fooling around here ...'

Lotte pouts, but she's afraid. She doesn't venture to say anything, she wouldn't be able to make a sound, her courage has disappeared all of a sudden, disappeared completely. Intimidated, she looks over to Erna. But to everybody's amazement Erika Tümmler starts talking suddenly, Erika Tümmler of all people! Who would have thought it!

Siodmak's secretary turns around, all the girls, and Lortzing too, can see her unchanged, composed face, the gently curving mouth with the expressive nose above it, and the strange eyes which never reveal what's really going on inside this girl, what she feels, thinks, wants … The slightly slanted eyes are shimmering a light green, transparent, clear, there's something enticing about them. Young men have looked into these eyes and then cried because they couldn't get what they wanted from this girl. They wrote stupid letters and did stupid things and were never able to forget Erika. But Erika has lots of things to forget.

She speaks very distinctly, and although she was born in Berlin and has lived in this city for twenty-six years, she has acquired the too-clear 'good' German which all the little girls who fight their way up learn.

Lortzing is breathing rapidly, he's panting, nothing like this has ever happened to him before.

But the girls are more shocked by Erika than by Lortzing.

Erika Tümmler says to him: 'Herr von Lortzing, we were just about to come and tell you that we're all stopping work until Trude Leussner is reinstated. You know very well why Trude Leussner hasn't been able to work as well recently as she did before, but maybe you don't know yet that she was taken to hospital this morning. These are our conditions, they're clear and self-explanatory. Also, we want to be paid at the legal rates.'

Erna, who is standing next to her, calmly hands the chalk-white Lortzing a carbon copy of the girls' ultimatum. In a truly eventful life, Herr von Lortzing has never experienced anything like this before, he stands there flabbergasted, with the ultimatum in his right hand. What is it that the Tümmler girl wants from him, they're threats, that's blackmail!

He stares at the ultimatum for a while without speaking, and then the other girls venture to look up again, they don't want to leave their leaders in the lurch at the start of the battle, something's stirring inside them, something's moving, a modicum of pride; they belong together, after all, and nobody should take a backward step. They recall the little humiliations which they have to put up with in this firm day after day. Their eleven faces are shining as they look over at the boss, faces which aren't really illuminated by a fighting spirit, faces dusted with powder, red mouths glowing, eyes gleaming with desire, but hardly the desire which sometimes seizes men before a hard battle, they have enticing hairdos in all kinds of colours, and you can read the fear of their own courage in their faces.

But Herr von Lortzing doesn't notice that fear.

He just says: 'I see, I see. You'll pay a high price for this!' and then turns around hurriedly and stumbles out, with the ultimatum still in his hand and a single bead of sweat on his forehead. His rage only breaks out in the corridor, he curses to himself as he strides back to his room. But he doesn't go to Siodmak yet, there's one particular thing which he has to think about carefully first.

But Erna assumes that Lortzing will rush straight off to his boss, she has to get in before him if she possibly can. She disappears promptly into the corridor, taking the other carbon with her. The words have been spoken now, the battlelines are clear, divided by the corridor, she's not afraid, only there's a hot feeling throughout her body, a balanced, strong, enthusiastic feeling, who knows what it is. These twelve or thirteen Berlin girls, she's only known them for a week, but already they're doing something big together, they're fighting together, they've got to win.

Erika catches her outside Siodmak's door.

'I'll give Siodmak our demands.'

Erna looks at her friend. She doesn't say anything, but her mouth is half-open, she disagrees.

Yes, Erika nods. She opens Siodmak's door and disappears into his room.

The solemn calm in the typists' room has been disturbed now, the silent expectation is a thing of the past, the girls are all speaking over the top of each other. They're not sitting in their chairs anymore, they're running around, they're asking questions, they're thinking, what's going on? What should we do? We've taken a risk, we can't go back now ...

This could be a good, determined mood, this could turn into a good, determined battle. Erna says nothing. She's conserving her strength, she's waiting. At one point, she thinks of Trude Leussner.

And she's just heard something, incidentally and without being noticed. When she came back into the typists' room, Lieselotte Kries was asking Eva Hagedorn: 'What did Erika mean when she said that we should be paid at the legal rates? Was it that Elfriede and Grete and Annemie are supposed to get as much as I do?'

Actually, the afternoon is surprisingly calm. Siodmak chucked Erika out of his room, that's all they hear of him, they don't even hear when he walks down the corridor and summons Herr von Lortzing to him.

It's only towards the end of the day that Erna sends some girls to the stairwell and the building at the front to keep a bit of a lookout. She doesn't think they'll find out anything important, she just wants to keep the girls occupied, because she soon sees that their enthusiasm is waning, their fear of their own boldness is rising again. A little patrol duty like this will freshen them up, encourage them.

In the meantime, Herr Siodmak is having a detailed conversation with Herr von Lortzing, and asks him who the ringleader is.

'This kind of thing doesn't come out of thin air! They weren't at all rebellious before. Have you ever spoken with the girls one at a time?'

And because Herr von Lortzing is required to give a satisfactory, clear and definite answer, he says promptly: 'That new girl, the little one at the Orga Privat …'

Siodmak leafs through a register.

'The Halbe girl … ? Dismiss her!'

Siodmak makes the call to the typists' room himself, summons his secretary Fräulein Tümmler to the phone and informs her that Fräulein Halbe is dismissed and must leave the premises immediately. And then, just this once, he won't punish anybody if the ladies resume their work immediately and make a special effort …

Then Fräulein Erika Tümmler, twenty-six years old, wearing a red silk dress, chic, young and hard to read, replies in her clear voice: 'You would do better to read our ultimatum!' and hangs up.

The girls look at Erika with expectant faces.

'Siodmak's scared already', she says, 'they can't get anything done without us.'

She doesn't say anything about Erna being dismissed.

That's the state of the battle on the afternoon of the first day.

When Erika calls out her 'Six o'clock!' in the typists' room as usual, the girls leave with a great deal of noise, but they're rather confused. They feel as if the trouble has passed now, and the typing can begin again tomorrow at the usual time. Haven't they forgotten something? They're conscious of a guilty feeling. Their eyes aren't aching from staring at their typewriters for hours, their joints aren't aching from sitting in their chairs for hours, they're not used to not working, they're not used to fighting. Maybe it's only the four girls on the action committee who can see the next step clearly, but Erika and Erna definitely know what's at stake. Everybody can see that they're directing the battle, consulting with each other, firing up the others. The girls go to them for advice and encouragement. Erika, the tall girl who always used to treat them coldly and dismissively and arrogantly, is undergoing a strange transformation. They're almost a bit afraid of her comradely attitude. They can't account for the turnaround.

But Erna Halbe is the soul of the struggle. She's a small girl, and clearly not very strong, she types on a wobbly Orga Privat and doesn't wear nice clothes, the girls once laughed at her because of that, she comes from the provinces, from some poky little place, nobody knows quite where, but they all take their cues from her.

After the other girls have gone, Erna and Erika stay in the typists' room, because Erika has to lock up. They've decided that all the girls should come back in the morning, punctually as always: the passive resistance will continue.

'Do you think we'll hold out?'

'Can we mobilize the building at the front?'

Many more employees of Iron Processing Co. – mainly male employees – work in the building at the front. But the two departments are kept strictly separate, they only know each other by sight.

'I'm meeting Fritz this evening, he'll go to the Central Association with me or to another of the unions, and they'll tell us what we have to do.'

'Are you worried about something?'

Erna tells her what Lieselotte said. She knows this flighty, unreliable girl better than anybody else, she knows how dangerous this is.

Erika laughs.

'We have to be prepared for that. If it all goes bad, then I'll just have to have another word with Siodmak. You see, he's different from Lortzing.'

'Oh, is he?'

'Yes, you need to get to know him personally. You might be surprised.'

Erika sits down on a desk. It's already getting dark outside. She can't see Erika's face clearly anymore.

'Fritz told me they were the most dangerous ones.'

'Yes, Siodmak can do what Lortzing can't: separate business and his private life completely. But it's not so easy to explain.' Erika starts humming to herself.

'So how's it been between you?' Erna is silent for a moment and then, when Erika doesn't answer, she adds: 'I mean, in private.'

'When you're with him, it doesn't feel at all like you're with your boss. He's pleasant and friendly, and he never talks about work. And that's why he never flirts with the girls in the office. I don't think he has a great deal of time for women. He has a big art collection that's his real passion. Old things, furniture, china and stuff like that. They say that his wife is still quite young, I don't know her. She's always travelling. From the Riviera to Switzerland, from there to Paris, but she hardly ever comes to Germany, let alone to Berlin. They have a kind of agreement. Each of them goes their own way.'

'So why did they get married?'

'Don't know.'

The building is completely quiet. Erna has folded her hands over her knees, which are pressed together. She swings her legs back and forth.

'If he's such a high-class guy, then I don't understand why he treats us so awfully.'

Erika laughs. 'I told you, he knows how to keep things nice and separate. We're part of the business, and we get paid. He probably has to account for that somewhere higher up in the company. His interest in us doesn't extend beyond that.'

'It extends to Erika Tümmler.'

'You're mistaken, Erna dear.'

Everything is quiet again. It's funny to be in such an empty, uninhabited building, hearing your own breathing, and nothing else. Erna would like to talk about something different, she already regrets starting this discussion. But Erika's face is completely shrouded by the darkness.

'Listen, I've got to tell you something else. The girls have no idea how sick Trude really is! I'm a bit scared, we should really go to visit her ...'

'Yes, I'll go over there this evening. You should just go through everything with your Fritz, and keep your chin up.'

'I should just? Do you really think that something can happen to me, of all people? Erika ...'

Erna puts out her right arm suddenly and touches her friend's shoulders. Then she decides to draw the girl to her, and holds her tightly in her arms. She tries to look into her eyes.

'You're not angry with me, are you?'

'You're the nicest girl I know.'

Erna lifts her right hand from Erika's shoulder, gently strokes her friend's face, her hair, tousles it tenderly, runs her fingers through it and draws Erika's head towards her, close, very close. Erika laughs softly, stops the movement by putting both hands under Erna's chin, lifts the little girl's face close to hers and gives her a rough, strong kiss. A pleasant, strong aroma remains on Erna's face.

When they leave the typists' room the bosses are nowhere to be seen, it's quiet behind all the doors. The girls' footsteps echo loudly in the corridors. Suddenly the telephone back in Lotte Weissbach's office starts ringing like a mad thing. The two girls look at each other. The corridor is asleep. The building is lonely and empty. The telephone wails again. In the offices of Iron Processing Co., Berlin, Prenzlau Avenue, in the middle of the city, a battle has begun. The ringing of the telephone dies away.

Erika locks the street door.

Aschinger's, Alexander Square.

Erna ran, so as to get there on time. The restaurant is very busy at this hour. People from the offices and shops, from department stores and workshops, travelling salesmen, taxi drivers, civil servants, policemen, young girls and suburban women, people who are staying in the city this evening, are taking a modest meal. Erna must be careful to avoid the waiters and waitresses, because she doesn't have any money. She can't even buy herself a sausage. And this evening, at the end of an eventful day, she feels really hungry. Of course, the small portions of dining-hall food don't get you through the day. Eighteen years old and no breakfast and no supper, that might not be enough. And today in particular she wants something good and hot and nourishing. Fritz is sure to have a bit of money left, or some bread and cold meat at home. Yes, Fritz is sure to give her something to eat. Maybe he'll order a couple of hot sausages. They'll sit at one of the little marble tables and eat very slowly. They've got time, they don't need to hurry. That will be so nice, everybody will see that we belong together, and I'll look happy the whole evening. But where can he be, it's already a quarter to seven. He's always late.

A fat man next to her is eating a couple of sausages, smacking his lips. He's staring fixedly in front of him, now and then he pushes a piece of sausage, daubed with mustard, into his moustache, which drips with fat as he chews. Erna has to look into this unpleasant man's face as it pushes down piece after piece of sausage, gurgling and smacking. Stupid thoughts come into her head, she wonders if it might be possible to marry the man. The man gets another portion, his third or fourth, and sits down next to Erna again. She's got to leave. She can't stand the sight of it anymore. She walks up and down outside Aschinger's a few times, she feels very cold all of a sudden. When it's almost seven o'clock she goes inside again. Fritz doesn't come. Naturally, she's angry at first, but gradually she becomes uneasy. Why is he keeping her waiting for so long? They were supposed to meet here, after all! And this is the only Aschinger's on Alexander Square. So where can he be? Maybe something's come up?

The gloomy day has been dispersed quickly by the evening, lovely cars are gliding gently through the damp streets, well-dressed women and elegant men are sitting in them, they're going to the theatre or out dancing in expensive clubs, the neon advertisements shine out and are reflected in the wet surfaces, countless signs with the names of businesses are lined up on parade, dead and pale on the lit-up façades. The noise of the street keeps on blaring into Aschinger's, shouts, footsteps, car horns, tram bells, screams, music, the sounds are all muted slightly and seem to come from far off... Tiredness is buzzing in her temples, and something's hammering in the back of her head, hunger and over-exertion and a slight anxiety are making their presence felt.

She waits until half-past seven, and then runs to Koppen Street. She rings, nobody opens the door.

Maybe he's standing outside Aschinger's now, she thinks. Her anxiety grows.

The repair shop is in Stralau Street, so she has to walk back a bit.

There's an old man still working in the office who doesn't know if and when the mechanic Fritz Drehkopf left.

'You'll have to ask in the garage', he says.

The man at the gate wants to chase Erna off, but she manages to walk through the big entrance into the workshop area, fortunately she runs into the mechanic Gustav Kliebein straight away, who's leaning on a hood, hands streaked with oil.

'Hello! Do you know Herr Fritz Drehkopf, Drehkopf the mechanic, I mean?'

The young man with the dirty face looks closely at Erna.

'Hey! Are you Drehkopf's girl?'

Erna nods, of course, who else?

Then Gustav Kliebein pushes himself off the hood, looks around, motions to Erna and walks to the back with her, into the toolshed. He takes her gently by the shoulders and looks at her searchingly.

'Lil' girl, it's good you've come straight to old Gustav. The cops've arrested Fritz …'

'What?'

'Yeah, it was a dirty business. I mean, he wanted to get his cash. Yeah, he talked with me first. Fritz, I said, don' do it like that. Well, the way he is, you'll know all about it, stubborn and so on, he just doesn' listen. Goes in, demands the money. They don' give him none, of course. He takes some from the till and gives the cashier a punch or two. The boss sends for the cops, the bastard says: Theft. Don' start crying, girl, if we'd known what was gonna happen Fritz'd still be here. He's probably in the lock-up in Moabit now.'

No, Erna's not crying at all, she's just staring into space, into space. Right. Fritz Drehkopf has been arrested. For theft. In Moabit … It's the poor what gets the blame.

Gustav Kliebein doesn't quite know how to deal with the girl. If she was crying, he'd be able to comfort her. But she's not saying anything, Fritz Drehkopf's girl. She's very pretty! If she needs somebody to keep her company in bed, then look no further: Gustav Kliebein, ninety-six kilograms, the best wrestler in the Fichte Club, unmarried, twenty-four years old and extraordinarily fit. He wouldn't take advantage of his pal Fritz at all, no, he just wants to be friendly. But because he can't quite work out what makes the girl tick, he keeps his specific suggestions to himself for the moment. He starts picking his nose in agitation. And it's just as well, because suddenly the little one dashes out of the toolshed without saying anything, without paying any attention when the man at the gate rushes out of his little cubicle, and disappears.

Cute as a bug, Kliebein thinks, Fritz has all the luck. They were some legs, a little bit supple at the knees, that's just what he likes. You'd kiss that girl like you mean business ...

Gustav Kliebein stands in the evening light like a figure in a dream, and eventually he realizes that and feels ashamed. Shit, he says loudly and clearly, and starts working on his motor again.

And Erna runs. She runs to the lock-up, she runs to Moabit, she runs from one room to another, she's looked at distrustfully, sent away, sent on to somebody else, again and again. Until finally she finds out that Herr Fritz Drehkopf, mechanic, Koppen Street, is in custody. He's in the building somewhere, accused of theft and damage to property; the first opportunity to visit him is Monday next week. No, I regret to inform you, any time earlier is impossible.

That's a hard thing to deal with at a hard time. Because Fritz was going to advise her, she's got to know how to carry on the battle, whether the unions will help, which steps should be taken. What can she do? Yes, now she alone has the responsibility, she alone has to guide the girls in the typists' room, fire them up, she alone must confront the management of Iron Processing Co., she must fight alone, it's only the victory which will be their collective achievement.

Of course, she mustn't say anything at the office about Fritz being arrested, these kinds of things discourage the girls, they're still so petit bourgeois about so many things, they wouldn't understand.

As Erna runs back to her apartment, a girl almost nineteen years old, she has never felt so isolated and alone in this city of Berlin. The people who pass her have suddenly become alien and unapproachable, they all have a family and a job and a life and a destiny of their own. Nobody turns to look at her, nobody will help her. Trams drive past her, the sound of their bells cuts through the night, it's shrill, barren and beast-like, the buildings look down on her with a freezing gaze, every one of them has a hundred signs and business names and advertisements, and none of the names offers her anything, no refuge, nowhere to call home. The river Spree flows darkly and silently on. No star shines above it. Yesterday the sky was full of them, no more, no more. The fear of those with nowhere to call home seizes her for a moment. Just for a moment, it must pass. She clenches her teeth and is suffused by a healthy defiance: DON'T GIVE IN!

In her apartment, everything is quiet, and nothing is moving in the Matscheks' part. In the light of the electric lamp her room looks alien and cold, but nothing has changed, nothing has been touched since that morning. Erna has had an eventful day in the meantime, and she's standing in her apartment for the last time, to say goodbye.

She leans a long way out of the open window. So she won't see that again, the embankment with the trains, the buildings with the firewalls, the sky with the clouds. Yes she will, she'll see all of it again, why should she forget the sky and the smoke from the trains? All of it will come back, even the night which has passed. She mustn't lose her courage in this great city of Berlin.

Erna looks slowly and thoughtfully around the room again. She looks at herself in the mirror, it's a good mirror. She can still sense the warmth of the previous night in the tumbled bedclothes. She packs up her few things. The gramophone downstairs is playing again. From the next room, where that Berger guy lives with the girl, she can hear sounds of tenderness. All the building's noises rush in to the lonely people who are lying on their beds unable to sleep, to the sick people whose fever can be seen in their wide eyes, to the restless people who are walking up and down.

Erna packs. She's soon finished and, just as on the first day, she stands there with the heavy suitcase and looks around. Then she has to think of the young man next door, what was his name again? Köhler, or something like that. He once said, it wasn't very long ago, come to me if you need help. Don't I need help now? she wonders. He's an honest boy, a Communist, he'll help me. But she doesn't really know, will he be able to tell her anything at all? Will he be able to think his way into the situation she's faced with?

She puts the keys on the garden table outside. The money isn't there, of course, the remainder of her month's rent. Very well, she thinks, then it's not there.

But the young worker from the apartment in the other corridor isn't at home, nobody opens the door when she knocks, and Erna walks down these stairs for the last time, her suitcase in her hand.

The dark night is blowing coldness down into the streets in swift gusts of wind, winter seems to be reaching its hand into the late spring again. Erna must move quickly through this night, it's already late to be walking with a heavy suitcase to Moabit. That's where Lotte Weissbach is renting a room. Erna has lots of time to think during the long walk, and she thinks about lots of things. She realizes that she's quite alone. Of course, Erika is standing beside her, and Lotte and maybe Trude and Elsbeth, but they're too soft, too careless in some ways, they have beautiful legs and enticing mouths, but they can't see beyond themselves, their attitude to this battle is unclear and contradictory. It's only Otti, that odd girl who doesn't worry particularly about all those things, whom Erna trusts. Otti is like her, she'll be able to rely on Otti.

When a little girl has to walk alone through the unfamiliar streets of the great city, and there are thoughts which she can chew on like a stick of gum, then lots of things become easier. She forgets. She can get her teeth into something in particular. There are lots of difficult problems which you can't solve straight away, and one of Erna Halbe's difficult things is the office she has to work in, and she thinks about the girls in the typists' room the whole time she's walking to Moabit. Actually, those girls live just as I do, she thinks. They've got boys they like, and that's how it should be. They have other boys, or men, who just pay for them when they go out somewhere, and that's just how it is. Because the men have the money, and they keep us away from it. And we all want to be happy, we want to get married and have children. And now we're fighting Iron Processing Co. Aren't the girls taking that seriously? Isn't a common cause taking shape already? Who got Erika involved in the battle? Do the other girls know who Erika is? I do, I know who she is. And Otti? Who is Otti? She's definitely a brave girl, but nobody knows that yet, because Otti hasn't shown them what she's capable of yet. If I'm firm and confident and uncompromising, if I say to them: Like this and like that, it's the only way to do it, if I never waver, then the girls will stick with me, then we'll win for sure.

She's moving fast. Once she has to ask for directions. And then she thinks about her girls again.

She almost forgets Fritz Drehkopf. Yes, she thinks, I love him very much, he's a good guy, and we'll always get on well with each other. A simple case of theft, no previous record, if it goes badly they'll lock him up for two months. Maybe he'll get a reasonable judge. But Fritz, dear, today and tomorrow and the day after I've got to think about something different and far more important, don't I? It's funny, everybody who would have helped me has been taken out of the game.

The walk to Moabit, carrying a heavy suitcase, seems to go on and on forever. Erna has a long time to think, and she needs it. The theatres are emptying, the people are hurrying home, Erna is marching her route. Past the station at Alexander Square, the one at the stock exchange, the one in Friedrich Street, the Lehrte, it's a nice long walk. Now and then she puts down the suitcase, takes quick, gulping breaths, and then she strides on swiftly and energetically.

She was here once already tonight, yes, in Moabit. Well, what does it matter. It'll be a new day tomorrow, the battle will continue. You've got to stay calm and confident, you can't get knocked off balance. And Erna reaches her destination.

Lotte and Martha aren't asleep yet. Only the child, a round-cheeked girl, is lying still and quiet in a hammock which is swaying in the darkest corner of the room, between a cupboard and some hooks for clothes.

'Now I'm here at last', Erna says to the two girls, with an apologetic gesture, 'Fritz couldn't come with me tonight, he's got the late shift, that's why it took so long. I had to carry everything by myself. But your building was easy to find, you've even got electric light in the entry.'

She takes off her hat and coat, smiling at Martha as she does so. Lotte is standing between them.

'No, what have you got to apologize for?'

Martha presses her hand, and they look at each other, and they laugh, and then Martha says: 'But you were late enough!' That's all she says, and all that needs to be said.

They have to talk quietly, so as not to wake the child. Lotte points to the hammock proudly, as if her own daughter was lying there. Strands of blonde hair are falling into the little girl's face, her sleep is tired but peaceful, her fists are pressed beneath her chin. Her lace nightdress is open at the front, a ridiculously slender, soft neck is peeping out, the child breathes deeply and shakes herself as she sleeps.

A red-and-white checked mattress cover is all the bedclothes in the hammock.

They turn off the lights, leaving on a little bedside lamp which spreads a subdued green glow.

'But you'll have to sleep on the sofa!' Lotte says.

The sofa has been transformed into a bed, already made up with sheets and blankets. Lotte and Martha will both sleep in the big bed, as they've been doing for a week.

Erna looks around, the room is surprisingly big, the four of them will be able to live together in it for a while.

'But you girls aren't allowed to bring your lovers home!' Lotte says. When two offended faces stare at her, she adds apologetically: 'I mean overnight.'

Erna doesn't say anything about Fritz Drehkopf. When she gives her opinion, she sometimes says: 'Fritz thinks so too.'

'If you knew how much I'd like to go to the office now, to be part of the whole thing! I've been fed up with Lortzing for ages. But listen – and I've already said this to Lotte too – you mustn't turn it into a personal fight, from beginning to end the story has to be: Typists Against Iron Processing Co.', Martha says.

'Of course, girl! It's obviously something that concerns all of us. What happens to Trude today can happen to any of us tomorrow. That's why I went a step further and added our demand to be paid at the legal rates.'

They talk about what to do next as they help Erna unpack, there's not much space left, the wardrobes and dressers are full, but there's room for everything provisionally. Lotte has to pay fifty marks rent without light or heating, they decide that each of them will contribute a third, and until Martha is working again Lotte and Erna will divide her third equally between them. After all, the situation is still quite complicated and uncertain, two are on strike, one is unemployed, apart from the fact that the police are looking for her, and they've got a child to look after as well. But they don't just need a roof over their heads, they have to eat and drink as well, they need clothes and shoes and lots of other things too. Maybe one of them will have some luck tomorrow or the day after, then she'll help the other two. They have to stick together, damn it, they have to be there for each other, they have to help each other, because there's no other way.

Late in the night, towards morning really, Erna wakes up. The room is still filled by the shadows of the night, except that there's a light shining from outside into the darkest corner, onto the hammock. The early noises are already starting up down there on the street: footsteps, cars are driving, milk cans are rattling. Erna squints, still half-asleep, she can hear the others breathing calmly, with different sounds, high and low, a strange, sleep-inducing noise. Something shifts in the hammock, the child speaks in a dream. Then Erna falls asleep again. But in the morning she's woken by little Martha, who has the same name as her mother. She looks at Erna with serious blue eyes and paws at her face. She's wearing a big pink ribbon in her thin hair. Erna lifts the little girl up and kisses her all over. Martha Hummel is boiling milk for her on the patent stove which belongs to the apartment.

'Up you get, lazybones', Martha says to Erna, who then greets Martha Hummel's little daughter: 'Well, you little cherub?'

Yes, the little girl looks radiantly healthy, but she doesn't talk very much, she's not together with other children very much, though she often sings to herself.

Erna does her duty, lifting little Martha above her head a couple of times, exclaiming at how much she weighs and how supple she is, and then they can drink coffee. The table is covered with a clean white cloth, there are rolls and butter, outside the sun is shining again, the day is starting well.

Now Erna meets Frau Pratt too, the pattern of a landlady. She rolls in, fat and comfortable, at least fifty years old, but with plaits curled up over her ears, which Erna finds extremely funny.

Lotte makes the introductions.

'Frau Pratt! … And Erna Halbe, The Girl at the Orga Privat!'

Frau Pratt bobs a bit at the knees.

'I hope you'll be happy here, Fräulein.'

God, what's Erna supposed to say!

'Just stay here until you can find your own apartment.'

Frau Pratt is supposed to drink coffee with the girls, but she doesn't have time, she has to go to the market. Fat and comfortable, with a friendly smile and her funny plaits, she takes herself off again.

'The one and only!'

'An angel!'

Martha junior has the last word: 'Aunty Pratt's a good one!'

Lotte puts red lipstick on her childlike mouth, powders over where the pillow pressed into her face, combs out her fringe, and then the two girls set off, having worked out their plan for the day and explained to Martha in detail where she can shop and how much she's allowed to spend. In this neighbourhood, she doesn't have to worry that somebody will know her and recognize her straightaway. But Wicleff Street, where she used to live, isn't too far away from her new home, and it's better to be safe than sorry.

Lotte and Erna say very little on the way to work, it's no small thing to be carrying the responsibility for a hard battle.

A few employees from the building at the front are standing outside on the pavement in Prenzlau Avenue, and they look at Erna and Lotte with interest. Aha, so word has already got around! The pair march past with swinging, decisive steps, their heads held high.

Yes, we're on strike! Take a good look!

Erika meets them in the corridor.

'Listen, I've been to see Trude, she's not doing well at all!'

'Wait, you should tell everybody everything as a report. We have to take care now that the girls stick together, otherwise we'll all get the sack at once.'

'Why? Are you really worried about that?'

'Safety first! And they should all hear the report about Trude.'

Elsbeth is playing a mouth organ which she took from her brother. She plays well, with rhythm. The girls are sitting in their chairs, as they do every day, they're clapping their hands in time with the mouth organ. Erna,

Lotte and Erika come in, everybody looks up. Erna feels how they move as one, how they're weighing her up, all at once she realizes quite clearly the responsibility resting on her. It's only a small campaign, a little group of ten or eleven girls in a single room who can be replaced by another eleven within an hour without much changing. But such movements grow overnight if their leaders are clear and confident.

'Listen, everybody! Elsbeth, put that thing away! Yes, yes, you play very well, but you've got to be quiet for a bit now. You elected us as your action committee, so of course you've got to listen to us and pay attention and trust us. I hope you understand that what we're doing here isn't very easy, and for anybody who hasn't worked that out yet, I'm telling you now. We mustn't ever let ourselves be discouraged and we've got to grab hold of every chance. We'll all stay here in the typists' room, and we won't touch any work – Understood? Erika and I will go over again, maybe they'll chuck us out this time too. We went to the Central Association of Office Workers last night ...'

That's not actually true, but Erna has to report something at all costs, has to encourage the girls at all costs. But she resolves to go there by herself this evening.

'... and they've said that they'll support us. So we've got some help there too. Then we'll have to send a few girls to the building at the front to do some advertising for us, especially in the records office and the typists' room, they'll be the easiest to get into. But the most important thing is: You've all got to keep your chin up ...'

Annemie Bergemann says pointedly: 'Well, it's all getting a bit boring!'

'Yes, children, if you thought that something like this was going to fall into your laps, you shouldn't have started it in the first place. I'm telling you quite clearly how things stand and what our chances are, so that nobody's in any doubt. Of course, Siodmak and Lortzing will play the tough guys for a while yet, they think we won't hold out for long and will knuckle under soon. Are we going to do what Siodmak and Lortzing want?'

'No!' two or three girls call out. 'Smash them! Stick to it!'

Later Erna sees Lieselotte Kries and Annemie talking animatedly to Vera. Aha, so there's a little group of strike-breakers already forming there.

Erna resolves to give these girls her particular attention, and plenty to do. She finds Lieselotte Kries's angry, anxious face particularly disturbing.

'Right, now be quiet for a moment. Erika went to see Trude at the hospital, she'll tell you how Trude's getting on.'

They're all attention, that interests them.

'Yes, it looks like Trude waited too long. They had to operate on her yesterday as soon as they admitted her, and she was still unconscious in the evening. I had to leave without seeing her. But this morning Trude's condition had deteriorated so much that there was no question of visitors being allowed in. Maybe this afternoon ...'

'So what's wrong with her?' Eva calls out.

'Something with her glands.'

Trude Leussner was always a bit proud and capricious, she kept to herself and didn't have much in common with the other girls. But she's been working in this office for years, she's known all the girls since the day they started. They're shocked now, when Erika tells them all this. They'd had no idea. There's a shadow standing in the room which won't go away. It's only now that they become properly furious with Lortzing, everything with them depends on their moods and their feelings. Erika's report makes them more determined. They're no longer as high-spirited and cheerful as they were in the morning, but they're more and more willing to fight. They decide that Eva and Elfriede will take flowers to the hospital at lunchtime. Elfriede takes a collection from the room, everybody gives a little bit, it's two marks twenty in total.

Suddenly, in the middle of all this, the internal telephone rings. The girls swivel around, they're quite frightened. Eva is closest, she has to push back her thick blonde hair before she can put the receiver to her ear.

'Us? Work? What? Not a chance ... Why don't you visit Fräulein Leussner in the hospital, see how she's doing? We have no intention of doing that ... What? You're going to dismiss us ... ? Hello! ... He hung up', she tells the girls, 'it was Siodmak.'

Everything goes quiet again, the girls have time to think about one thing and another, and that's dangerous. A wage fight like this one, in a ridiculously small place, typists' room in the building at the back, thirteen employees with no representatives on a management committee, none of them union members, and all of them girls too, about twenty years old, with strange desires and big hopes, cheeky, courageous, but a bit lightweight and careless too, a bit soft and uncertain, a bit too petit bourgeois, a fight like this one is in danger of people deserting the whole time, of running from the battle, of betraying the cause. People are already venturing to complain here and there, Lieselotte is hammering demonstratively on her keyboard, she's sitting there, pouting and gloomy, because Erika criticized her. Erika wants to put things right again, she's a real help to Erna. Normally you never see her in the typists' room, but now she's putting herself at the centre. She's standing right next to Erna. She's brought a book with her, and the girls are reading aloud from it in turn. *The Sea-Wolf* by Jack London. The boredom isn't so terribly oppressive anymore.

Otti bursts in, little Ottilie Heynicke. She was snooping around outside, and discovered something. A girl from the building at the front.

'That's what you get!' Otti says, full of reproach.

The girl, a peroxide blonde who comes in calmly, rather surprised and very curious, tells her story again.

'Your Siodmak telephoned our office manager. He needs somebody temporarily for dictation. Well, the office manager sent me over. It's not my fault!'

'Nah,' Elfriede says, 'but go back home now like a good girl!'

Erna explains everything to the girl.

'Yes, yes, we know it all already', she replies.

'But you don't want to stab us in the back, surely. I mean, you can say we didn't let you through.'

The girl takes herself and her steno pad off.

Lieselotte complains.

'But you've got to let the girl go to Siodmak. It's not right. It's practically Bolshevism …'

'What kind of talk is that? What kind of talk is that? Are we supposed to offer ourselves to your dear Herr Siodmak? Have you got a screw loose somewhere?'

The argument goes back and forth.

But in the meantime, Otti draws up a sentry roster which includes each girl in turn.

'And we'll send a second girl with Lieselotte', Erna says, 'so that she doesn't cheat us.'

Erika reads out the next section of *The Sea-Wolf*.

And Erna draws Lieselotte out into the corridor.

'Come on, I've got something to tell you.'

Lieselotte looks quite reluctant, maybe she's ashamed of herself. She just says Yes and Of course to everything, nodding all the time. The conversation doesn't satisfy Erna in the least.

A hot day. The silence in the room becomes even more palpable against the background of the even, monotonous voices of the girls who are reading aloud. Flies buzz around the silent typewriters, the girls have propped their chins on their hands or are swinging back and forth on their chairs. Annemie Bergemann is clearly asleep. But she is jerked awake. The door bangs open, that can't be a girl coming in. Lotte, who happens to be reading, closes the book in surprise. Because it's the director, Herr Siodmak, creased, fat, with prominent little piggy eyes, his hands in his trouser pockets. He's wearing a beautiful dark brown suit, the creases are shining, he always dresses very carefully. Everything is quiet for a time. The girls stare at their boss. He's smiling, that's what's uncanny. He smiles calmly and gently for a time. Then his rough voice lets rip. A few of the girls are sitting like small animals entranced by the gaze of the snake which is about to swallow them.

'I see that you've made yourselves comfortable. Can one of the gracious ladies perhaps tell me what's the meaning of this?'

Erna has heard that tone before. She makes her move.

'Why did you dismiss Fräulein Leussner?'

'Hold your tongue. I have no intention of speaking to you. You were dismissed a long time ago. You're trespassing here, do you understand?'

The girls look up, look from Siodmak to Erna, who's standing next to her Orga Privat, small, pale and brave. It's such a fascinating situation, he's really letting himself go. It seems to be getting serious now.

'I'll give you one more chance, although you've done nothing to deserve it. If you start working again immediately, I'll forget about what's happened today. I'll have a day's pay deducted from your salaries. Otherwise, I suppose Fräulein Tümmler knows where your papers are kept in my office.'

The girls' hearts are beating rapidly and fearfully. But the boss's secretary, Fräulein Erika Tümmler, steps calmly towards him and snaps her fingers in the air.

'Herr Siodmak, we want Fräulein Leussner's unfair dismissal to be withdrawn, and the other little demands in our manifesto to be granted. Then we'll start work again immediately. That's really not too much. And we can't accept any disciplinary measure against Fräulein Halbe.'

'I see. Then I demand that you leave the premises. As sorry as it makes me, you are all dismissed. We'll see each other again at the Labour Tribunal. Good day!'

Bang, the door is closed.

The girls look at each other, in silence, for a long time. Eva comes in from sentry duty and enquires what Siodmak wanted here. And then the story has to be told again to Grete Theier, who had gone to buy a bunch of windflowers for Trude. The atmosphere in the room is very chastened. *The Sea-Wolf* was dropped under a cupboard in the first moment of fright, and it stays lying there.

Annemie Bergemann is almost crying, she says that Erika has gone much too far, the police will come now and the court …

Some of the girls are already wavering, or at least they think Erika's sharp tone wasn't right, and Lieselotte suggests that Erika should apologize. Siodmak's elegant secretary is sitting quietly on a desk, swinging her long legs, saying nothing at all.

And then Erna bursts out, she's got to say something now, she's the leader here, she bears the responsibility here. And what would Fritz Drehkopf say if he heard how shamefully the struggle had ended? Grit your teeth, and don't think about the little personal injuries, stick it out …

'… You're letting him bluff you! You just fall right down as soon as Siodmak breathes on you. Of course we'll stay here, and we won't give in. And the unions are behind us! We'll have lunch now, I'll go to the Central Association again, and then we'll know what to do next …'

'You'll always know what to do next and you always know better than us', Lieselotte bursts out all of a sudden, 'but after they've sacked us nobody will help us, then it'll be up to us to find another job. We'd be fools not to give in. I can tell you all that I'm starting to work again …'

'Nobody's starting! And you're not either, Lieselotte! Are you really going to stab us in the back? Haven't I always said that a bit of courage, a bit of endurance, is part of it? We don't need scared little mice! Come on, think of Trude! She's in hospital now, and do you all know why? Because Herr von Lortzing got the pleasure, and doesn't want to get the blame! That's right, you can all stare at me. You know what I mean. Anybody who breaks ranks now, when not even the girls in the building at the front are going to let us down, is a cowardly little scoundrel. And it seems there are some of you who haven't got their fingers quite burned yet. I hope that's enough.'

Erna is furious, she's been looking angrily at Lieselotte, she doesn't care what happens.

Erika is still swinging her legs, she's gone so far as to light a cigarette, she's contemplating her openwork shoes, smiling and intent.

Annemie Bergemann is still anxious.

'But he said you've been dismissed. What does that mean?'

Yes, nobody knows what that's supposed to mean.

Erika swings her legs, smiles, and says nothing.

Eva is already putting on her coat.

'Come on', she says to Elfriede, 'let's get the bus to the hospital, so that we get back in good time.' And to the other girls she says: 'Erna's right. You haven't even started properly yet, and you're giving up already.'

'Who's giving up?' Lotte Weissbach asks. 'Do you mean me, by any chance?'

Erika isn't smiling anymore, she knows that they've got past another obstacle, the battle will go on for a while longer. But how long? Who will hold out the longest?

'You'll be back on the dot of three, understood?'

Erika and Lotte and Elsbeth and Erna go to lunch together. When they reach the door of the dining hall, Erna realizes that they've done something stupid.

'We should have left a few girls in the office.'

'What for?'

'Yes, that definitely would have been better.'

'Listen, tomorrow's Sunday, you can't sit there then as well.'

'That's right, but … Hey, what's that?'

Their regular table, more or less in the middle of the dining room, is festooned with flowers, violets and lilies of the valley and even a bunch of lilacs.

'That can't be for us.'

But the boys and girls at the tables are clapping their hands, the quartet from Iron Processing Co. are being admired from all sides.

'Is that our table?' Elsbeth asks disbelievingly.

The boys are still clapping, and the girls are looking their way, and the owner is already bringing the soup. The red-headed girl is standing in front of them in an elegant white kasha satin blouse and a short blue skirt, a gentle smile on her face, and she hands Erna a little parcel wrapped in crackling paper.

'The regular customers organized a little collection for the strikers at Iron Processing Co. and hope that you'll continue your battle and win.'

She says this quite slowly, word by word, in a clear, pleasant voice to four astonished girls.

'How did you all know about it?'

'It's the kind of thing that gets around.'

The traveller in cosmetics is there again too. He permits himself to remark that there will probably be a report about their struggle in that evening's edition of the Communist Party's newspaper.

Erna expresses thanks on behalf of Iron Processing Co.'s employees, stuttering for the first time. The little parcel is still on the table in front of her. The food tastes wonderful to the girls today, the owner has put much more than usual on the plates too, and Erna gets soup and dessert even though she's only paid for 'without'.

The red-headed Hilde and the young people point out the heroines to new guests. It's a very cheerful lunch, with all kinds of threatening remarks about Iron Processing Co.

'It's a pity', Elsbeth says, 'that Lieselotte's not here …'

'And all the others too', Lotte adds.

When they're about to leave, Erika embraces the red-headed girl.

Once they're outside, they count the money.

Sixteen marks fifty, mostly in fifty-pfennig pieces.

'What'll we do with it?'

'Well, everybody will have to decide that, of course. The best thing would be to put it aside as a reserve.'

'Sixteen-fifty?' Lotte asks doubtfully.

'I suppose that's not enough for you?'

They get back to Prenzlau Avenue earlier than usual, but Lieselotte and Annemie and Vera are already standing there, cursing. The misfortune which Erna sensed has happened: The door to the typists' room, all the doors except the one to the administration office, are locked. And the door to the administration office leads to Siodmak's room.

'Bang', Elsbeth says, 'now we're all standing here.'

'Yes, now you're all standing here! First you let us slide into the dirt, now you don't know what to do, you're ...'

'Lieselotte, hold your tongue, understood?!'

Erna speaks sharply, without caring about Lieselotte's feelings, the victory isn't at stake anymore, they've probably lost. The girls' livelihoods are at stake now.

'We'll stay outside here. Erika and I will go in to Siodmak again. But first you've got to decide if we'll break off the fight. No, let me finish. Then everybody can say what she thinks, and we'll vote. But if anybody is rude to another girl, she'll be in trouble. I'd say that we're all in the same boat, nobody's better off or worse off.'

The girls nod in agreement, yes, that's how it should be done. But Eva and Elfriede aren't back from the hospital yet, and of course they've got to be part of it.

The atmosphere in the passageway of the building at the back is uncertain. Elsbeth fetches the big wooden bench from the foyer, some girls sit down, the others stand along the wall. The sunlight doesn't come in this far, the corridor is filled with shadows and a twilight coolness. A clock strikes in a distant room, sometimes you can hear the car horns tooting outside. Elsbeth tells a joke, and nobody laughs. The silence becomes more and more unpleasant and oppressive, not a sound comes from Siodmak's or Lortzing's room. The girls are alone.

'Well', Lieselotte says, 'we can't wait until Eva and Elfriede come back.' Her weepy voice makes a high, unpleasant sound in the corridor. She's wearing something new again, a sporty blue sweater.

'I'll tell you all what I think. I mean, we're stenotypists for Iron Processing Co., we're not factory girls, but what we're doing here is the kind of thing the Communists and people like that do, and that's not our kind of thing at all. Siodmak's not the worst boss by a long way, and I've always got something when I asked for it. I went in in a friendly way and spoke with the gentlemen, and they were always friendly and obliging to me …'

These sharp and bitter words are spoken by a twenty-two-year-old girl with nothing unique about her, she's a typical case. At the beginning, she was isolated; when the enthusiasm waned, girls started listening to her. Now all the thoughts and feelings that were pent up during an afternoon and a morning and the night in between are pouring out of her. The girls are listening to her with attentive, anxious expressions, and most of them are being infected by her panic. Erna and Erika are among the calm ones, they have a different motive, they're still following their path, they won't listen to this provocative speech to the end, they'll step in, maybe Erna is already opening her mouth, maybe Erika is already saying something, but all of them, all three of them fall silent, because something new, something incomprehensible happens.

Somebody is sobbing. Somebody is walking up to them slowly and sobbing.

'Who's that?'

'Hello!'

'Eva?'

'What are you crying for, Eva?'

Thirteen girls worked for Iron Processing Co., two secretaries and eleven typists. But there are only seven stenotypists standing in the corridor now. Two have just come from the hospital, the police are looking for one for abducting a child, and one …

'Trude has died.'

'What?'

'What did you say?'

'Elfriede, that can't be true!'

'Have you come from the hospital?'

'How can that have happened?'

'Trude?'

'But she was here just yesterday morning!'

Trude Leussner, twenty years old, brave, courageous, full of dreams, died shortly before eleven o'clock on Saturday morning following her second surgery, the last attempt to deal with the complications from a botched operation. However much she regretted her miserable little fate, she didn't die in vain.

The girls can't doubt that what Elfriede says is true, and they can't understand it. Eva and Elfriede are standing among them with tears on their faces, they saw the body. The girls feel as if Trude was a casualty in the battle between the typists' room and Iron Processing Co., the first casualty.

Can the girls understand how one of them wants to sabotage their struggle with her little problems and concerns?

Erika takes Eva gently by the shoulder.

'Come on, don't cry anymore. I'm going over to Siodmak.'

She has tears in her eyes, two bright silver stars. She leaves quickly and goes to the back of the building.

The other girls remain in the corridor, not knowing what to do next. Erna stares into Elfriede's tear-stained eyes. Can Elfriede really mean it? Erna is the only one who knew how sick Trude was, but she didn't believe it was that bad. How can it have happened? That Trude's existence has been wiped out, blown away …

The other girls have formed a tight, attentive circle around Eva and Elfriede, they have to tell the story. What did Trude look like? Much changed? What did the doctors say? Were her parents there?

Everybody knows something about Trude, she was always a bit standoffish, didn't really have a proper friend in the office, but each of them had had some experience or other with her. Trude was one of them, now she's dead. They fought for the dead girl, they're still fighting. The girls feel something good and strong, their battle has a purpose, they'll have to fight it to the finish, it won't have been in vain.

They don't know how long they've been waiting now. They can't cry anymore, and they don't want to cry. There are more important things to do. They look at Erna. The little girl stands calmly among them, left hand on hip. The corridor is getting cooler, evening is coming, the noise outside is increasing. They'll go out and they'll work again, they'll enjoy themselves, they'll love and they'll be disappointed, the girls of Berlin.

Erna turns around.

Lortzing's door is unlocked from the inside, he himself comes out, shoots past them without a word and disappears into Siodmak's office. He doesn't look at the girls.

'Siodmak will have telephoned him', Erna suggests. Lieselotte Kries comes up to her, looking miserable.

'If I'd known that Trude was so sick I swear I wouldn't have been against you all.' Lieselotte feels herself backed into a corner, she's shocked, she sees that she's on her own, badly on her own. But the other girls have a hot gleam in their eyes, their pulses are racing, their cheeks are glowing, the pain has brought them together again and united them. Now they know what they're standing here and waiting for …

'I know I behaved badly, I thought …'

Erna interrupts her crisply.

'Leave that now.'

Erika comes back. She waves to Erna.

'You're to come over with me.'

'I am?'

'Yes. Siodmak wants to talk to you.'

'Really.'

They stay close to each other as they walk down the narrow corridor.

'So what does he want from me?'

'Just go in. You'll know what you have to say.'

Erika knocks. They both go into Siodmak's room. Lortzing isn't there anymore, he's probably next door.

Siodmak is sitting at the desk, he looks closely at the little girl Erna as she walks in unconcernedly, with long strides and swinging arms. She stops in the middle of the room. Erika leans on the door, puts her head back and contemplates the ceiling.

'Fräulein Halbe, you're new here. Yes. We met each other once before. And what have you done?'

What can Erika have told him, Erna thinks, looking at him calmly. After a while he continues.

'Fräulein Tümmler has informed me of the regrettable fact that Fräulein Leussner has died. Yes, well, do you think that's our fault?'

He stubs out his cigar without taking his eyes off Erna. Those eyes are cold, small, dangerous, but his voice is conciliatory. So what does he want from me, Erna wonders.

'Please give me the keys to the typists' room', Erika says suddenly, 'so that the girls don't have to stand in the corridor.'

Siodmak promptly takes a bunch of keys from his trouser pocket, detaches one and gives it to Erika, who disappears immediately. Erna and Siodmak are alone.

'Do you know that we've dismissed you? No? But I made the phone call myself. Odd business. Well, let's leave that. Please be honest for once. Did somebody give you an order to start a rebellion amongst the girls?'

He's speaking in a calm, considered manner in a friendly, fatherly voice. Erna's lips pucker, her eyes become big and round, then she answers just as calmly and carefully.

'We didn't want to leave Trude Leussner in the lurch, that's all, and we were right.'

'You spoke with Fräulein Leussner, didn't you? You were friends with her?'

'Yes.'

'I don't know what Fräulein Leussner told you, but you can rest assured that both Herr Lortzing and I acted perfectly correctly. In every respect.'

There's a big window behind Siodmak's desk, Erna looks out of it while he's speaking to her. There's a huge brick building opposite, immersed in the grey light of the late dusk. Lights are going on in the windows, people are working there too, Berlin has a hundred thousand offices, one thing and another happens in them, good things and bad, everything looks so simple and normal, so uncomplicated, and yet mysterious things happen everywhere. The moon swims through the clouds, night and day change over. Everybody goes on, wearing the same face. There's a little girl standing here, it's evening, decisions are being made, small matters, big ones. Berlin, Prenzlau Avenue.

'I'm very sorry, but of course I can't retain your services. Our prestige in your colleagues' eyes demands that we adhere to your dismissal. I'll make you a suggestion: We'll pay you a full month's salary, and you'll look for another position. And we'll give you a reference as well, of course. We'll phrase it in a way which doesn't create any difficulties for you. You're sure to find another position soon.'

What's she supposed to say? Erna is silent. Her face is barely visible anymore in the gloomy room, you can only sense the outlines of her small figure.

'You can't begin to imagine the difficulties which the cessation of work has already created for us. Letters have been left unanswered. And I'm responsible. I've just been informed that an important long-distance call from our board of directors wasn't put through. You don't realize such things.'

There's a knock on the door. Erika comes in again.

'Fräulein Tümmler, please take the documents with you right away. The girls can start work again. I think we've reached an agreement.'

The two girls leave. Siodmak lights himself a fresh cigar. He stays sitting in the dark for a while, staring in front of him. Then he shakes his head. 'Strange girls', he says. His words sound quite odd. Metal strikes on metal in the central heating, making a high, chirping sound. The janitor is probably working in the basement. Apart from that, everything in the room is quiet.

'What did he want?' Erika asks.

'You're all supposed to start work again.'

'We're all? Aha, you've got the sack, haven't you?'

'Erika, listen to me, I've got something important to say to you. I think now is the most favourable moment to break off the fight, because we won't get anything more. No, listen to me. You've got to understand one thing: the girls might still stick it out today. Tomorrow's Sunday, on Monday they're certain to be tired of the fight, and they definitely won't stick it out any longer than Tuesday. But the Labour Office will probably have sent enough girls here by Monday morning. It's obvious that Siodmak can hold out longer, you'll have realized that too. He's giving us a chance. That's how he's squaring his conscience. Who knows what our position would be if Trude was still alive. Trude's death probably saved us …'

'Erna, I know all that, but we can't let you be the scapegoat.'

'And the day after tomorrow, you'll all be sacked! No, Erika, you don't need to worry about me, it's not so bad. I don't think I'm sacrificing myself for all of you, that would be childish, but there's no other way. And anyway, Siodmak's going to give me my full month's salary, and I'll have a new job long before I've spent that. Don't you think so too?'

They stand in the corridor. All that can be seen in the darkness is Erika's white silk blouse, which still smells fresh from the wash. It feels odd that Trude isn't with them anymore. And now Erna Halbe is going to disappear too. Do these things matter so much?

They look at each other, they understand each other. Erika touches the little girl whom she doesn't really know gently on the neck. She's much taller, and with a motherly gesture she draws Erna to her, into her arms. Their faces touch, they just brush briefly, for a moment. Erika is wearing Houbigant, the smell of her perfume clings to Erna, she'll still think about it sometimes.

'Right. Now you've got to tell the girls.'

Erika leads the way.

The girls are all sitting in their chairs, they haven't put on the lights yet, the typists' room is quiet and sad.

Erika starts talking softly.

'Listen to what we've got for you, everybody. We're supposed to start working again, nothing will happen to us, only Erna's going to be dismissed.'

'No', Elsbeth cries out, 'I won't be part of that, if only Erna's going to be thrown to the wolves …'

Erna interrupts, saying that it's simply a question of tactics, she'll find another job alright. And Siodmak has guaranteed to pay her a full month's salary, that's a concession as well. She says that they have to put an end to the battle now, even if it's clear that they haven't won a complete victory. But it's not a capitulation, just a withdrawal. And they should learn from it that solidarity is a great and a wonderful thing.

The girls sit there, apathetically and tearily. Lieselotte Kries is lying on her desk, her head resting on her forearms. She's still crying, she won't settle down.

It turns out that three of the girls are opposed to breaking off the fight on these terms: Elsbeth Siewertz, Lotte Weissbach and Otti Heynicke. They don't want to let their little friend at the Orga Privat be the scapegoat. On the evening of the second day of struggle, the passive resistance is broken off.

THUS ENDS THE STORY OF THIS BATTLE, THE BATTLE WHICH HAS NO END.

Erna Halbe, a little working-class girl, defiant and determined, from healthy stock and with the right kind of hatred, takes her leave of her friends at Iron Processing Co. Every one of them shakes her hand.

'Goodbye!' they say.

'Come back soon!'

And she says: 'Don't you forget me!'

She leaves the typists' room, with the order to pay her salary in her hand. Behind her, as dusk descends on the cool building, the typewriters are already starting to clack away again. Her Orga Privat is silent. She walks out into this unfamiliar city, to Alexander Square, through the centre, to Potsdam Square. Confident and unmoved, in a nice white voile dress, her prominent nose pointing proudly forward, a gentle light in her green eyes, she marches on. Fritz Drehkopf is in prison, he'll get out again, she's been dismissed, she'll find a job again. The world's suffering isn't so great when the working people help each other, when comradeship and resistance grow within their ranks. One woman can't do anything. One woman can do a lot.

She disappears from our sight into the evening confusion of Berlin's streets, on her way to the nearest Labour Office. Car horns sound, the elevated trains rumble past, you can hear typewriters clacking away through the open office windows, a tumultuous noise fills the city, Berlin is working.

Unsullied, with a healthy instinct and a clear head, she put an end to a battle in which there was nothing more to gain. But the battle hasn't ended yet.

She disappears from our sight, into the confusion.

The girls in the typists' room at Iron Processing Co. will continue their work. Sometimes one of them will say something about Erna, with secret pride and undisguised love. The days will pass, become weeks, months. New girls will come into the office, and they'll all be told little stories about Erna

Halbe, little things she said, she'll continue to live among them. Her name will fade slowly. What she did won't be forgotten, it will grow and grow.

But her name faded away, and because eventually nobody remembered it anymore, the heroine of this story was called what she was called at the beginning:

THE GIRL AT THE ORGA PRIVAT.

German Studies in Australia and Aotearoa New Zealand

The series publishes scholarly works in the field of German Studies. It is aimed at profiling scholarship that has been produced in Australia and Aotearoa New Zealand. The series accepts submissions in German or English across the full spectrum of scholarship, ranging from doctoral dissertations and monographs to anthologies and collected essays. The series is edited by Tim Mehigan (University of Queensland).

Volume 1 Dushan Stankovich: Otto Julius Bierbaum
– eine Werkmonographie
1971. ISBN 978-3-261-00327-0

Volume 2 David Roberts: Artistic Consciousness and Political Conscience
– The Novels of Heinrich Mann 1900–1938
1971. ISBN 978-3-261-00328-7

Volume 3 Anthony R. Stephens: Rilkes Malte Laurids Brigge
– Strukturanalyse des erzählerischen Bewusstseins
1974. ISBN 978-3-261-00888-6

Volume 4 Margaret Stoljar: Athenäum: A Critical Commentary
1974. ISBN 978-3-261-01067-4

Volume 5 John Milfull: From Baal to Keuner: The 'Second Optimism' of Bertolt Brecht
1974. ISBN 978-3-261-01015-5

Volume 6 Ernst Keller: Kritische Intelligenz: G.E. Lessing – F. Schlegel – L. Börne: Studien zu ihren literaturkritischen Werken
1976. ISBN 978-3-261-01674-4

Volume 7 Anthony R. Stephens, H. Leslie Rogers and Brian Coghlan (eds): Festschrift for Ralph Farrell
1977. ISBN 978-3-261-01637-9

Volume 8 Reinhard Alter: Gottfried Benn: The Artist and Politics (1910–1934)
1976. ISBN 978-3-261-01871-7

Volume 9 E.L. Marson: The Ascetic Artist: Prefigurations in Thomas Mann's *Der Tod in Venedig*
1979. ISBN 978-3-261-03120-4

Volume 10 Steven R. Fischer: The Dream in the Middle High German Epic: Introduction to the Study of the Dream as a Literary Device to the Younger Contemporaries of Gottfried and Wolfram
1978. ISBN 978-3-261-03138-9

Volume 11 Sybil Hitchman: The World as Theatre in the Works of Franz Grillparzer
1980. ISBN 978-3-261-04615-4

Volume 12 Roger Hillman: Zeitroman: The Novel and Society in Germany 1830–1900
1983. ISBN 978-0-8204-0010-5

Volume 13 Gregory B. Triffitt: Kafka's 'Landarzt' Collection: Rhetoric and Interpretation
1985. ISBN 978-0-8204-0204-8

Volume 14 Peter H. Oettli: Tradition and Creativity: The Engelhard of Konrad von Würzburg: Its Structure and its Sources
1986. ISBN 978-0-8204-0302-1

Volume 15 Gerhard Schulz, Tim Mehigan und Marion Adams (Hrsg.): Literatur und Geschichte 1788–1988
1990. ISBN 978-3-261-03994-1

Volume 16 Rachel Jakobowicz: Jews and Gentiles: Anti-Semitism and Jewish Assimilation in German Literary Life in the Early 19th Century
1992. ISBN 978-3-261-04460-0

Volume 17 Rodney W. Fisher: Heinrich von Veldeke: *Eneas*
1992. ISBN 978-3-261-04538-6

Volume 18 David Scott: Metaphor as Thought in Elias Canetti's *Masse und Macht*
1999. ISBN 978-3-906759-09-8

Volume 19 Geoff Wilkes: Hans Fallada's Crisis Novels 1931–1947
2002. ISBN 978-3-906770-32-1

Volume 20 Richard Millington: Snow from Broken Eyes: Cocaine in the Lives and Works of Three Expressionist Poets
2012. ISBN 978-3-0343-1069-7

Volume 21 Lukas Bauer: The South in the German Imaginary: The Italian Journeys of Goethe and Heine
2015. ISBN 978-3-0343-1920-1

Volume 22 Anita Perkins: Travel Texts and Moving Cultures: German Literature and the Mobilities Turn
2016. ISBN 978-3-0343-2218-8

Volume 23 Geoff Wilkes (ed.): The Girl at the Orga Privat: A Short Novel from Berlin
2024. ISBN 978-1-80374-532-9

Milton Keynes UK
Ingram Content Group UK Ltd.
UKHW021509021224
3319UKWH00042B/1030